WOMEN GIFTED FOR MINISTRY

HOW TO DISCOVER
AND PRACTICE YOUR SPIRITUAL GIFTS

D1451076

WOMEN GIFTED FOR MINISTRY

HOW TO DISCOVER
AND PRACTICE YOUR SPIRITUAL GIFTS

Ruth and Elmer Towns

Publishers Since 1798

Thomas Nelson Publishers
Nashville

Published in Nashville, Tennessee, by Thomas Nelson, Inc.

Unless otherwise noted, Scripture quotations are from THE NEW KING JAMES VERSION. Copyright © 1979, 1980, 1982, 1990, Thomas Nelson, Inc. Scripture quotations noted NIV are from the HOLY BIBLE: NEW INTERNATIONAL VERSION®. Copyright © 1973, 1978, 1984 by International Bible Society. Used by permission of Zondervan Publishing House. All rights reserved. Scripture quotations noted TLB are from THE LIVING BIBLE, copyright © 1971. Used by permission of Tyndale House Publishers, Inc., Wheaton, Illinois 60189. All rights reserved. Scripture quotations noted KJV are from the KING JAMES VERSION.

Library of Congress Cataloging-in-Publication Data available from Library of Congress

Towns, Ruth and Elmer Towns
   Women gifted for ministry: how to discover and practice your spiritual gifts
ISBN 0-7852-4599-5

Printed in the United States of America

1 2 3 4 5 6 – 06 05 04 03 02 01

CONTENTS

A WOMAN'S TOUCH

I like this book for several reasons, and I know you will like it too. First, it believes in women and tells us we are gifted by God and can be used by God. If you've ever had self-doubts and wondered if you could be used by God, this book is for you. It teaches that all of us have gifts and God wants to use us.

There's a second thing you'll like about this book: It shows that one of the reasons for the differences between women is their different talents. Ruth and Elmer call it "gift mix." God has given us different gifts in different degrees of effectiveness. That makes you different from all other women. You already know that we are different in the clothes we wear and the way we wear them. Our makeup is different, as are our hairstyles and the way we decorate our homes. Read this book to find out what different gifts you have and then discover what you can do with your abilities.

You'll love the stories of women in the Bible. Ruth and Elmer have highlighted nine different women in the Bible by their spiritual gifts. Then they have included stories of contemporary women and how they used their gifts to serve God.

I think this will make a wonderful Bible study book for your Sunday school class or home Bible study. There are many practical, hands-on learning experiences at the end of each chapter. Then, you must take the Spiritual Gift Questionnaire at the end of the book. Most of you already know what your gifts are, but taking this questionnaire will give you confidence about your gift and will help you mentor others into service for Christ. But some of you who read this book have never thought of spiritual gifts and you don't know what your gifts are. You'll know yourself better when you finish working your way through this book.

Ruth and I have been friends for over twenty years. You'll meet her in this book and love her as I do. I wish you could visit her home; she'd make you feel comfortable, because that's a good word to describe Ruth. She has a comfortable home and she would make you feel prized just by a visit.

Over the years, Elmer has bought Ruth stuffed bears from his travels around the world. She has over three hundred teddy bears and they are all in a guest room where John and I have stayed. It is a "beary" comfortable room with bears everywhere.

Ruth is the only woman I've ever known to have a white living room: white rugs, walls, stuffed furniture and a white baby grand piano. Then there's a "white-on-white" gigantic oil painting over the fireplace; it, too, has white birch logs and white-handled andirons. I think a white room reflects the "pure" spirit I sense in Ruth.

Enjoy your reading. Learn! Experiment with your gifts. Grow in Christ. Then go out and serve the Lord better.

Sincerely yours,

Margaret Maxwell

INTRODUCTION

FIND YOUR GIFT— FIND YOUR MINISTRY

I (Ruth) had my life turned around by a Sunday school lesson taught by Elmer in the early '80s. He presented a lesson on the spiritual gifts taught in Romans 12:3–8. I knew about spiritual giftedness and knew gifts were given for Christians to serve God, but I never really thought about my spiritual gift. I just saw myself as one who had God's help when I served Him. That morning, Elmer identified the seven spiritual gifts with seven people in our church. Associating each person with his or her dominant spiritual gift, he said I had the gift of mercy-showing, and that I was one of the best counselors that he knew. Elmer said three things about me: First, I always took time from other tasks to counsel people who had problems; second, God had used me in counseling; and third, counseling was my greatest gifted ability. I had never thought of myself as a counselor until he said it, although I knew I liked to help people.

That Sunday school lesson changed my life. On the way home, I said to him, "If I am such a good counselor, what am I doing selling real estate?" Elmer said I had to answer that for myself. I did!

I determined that I loved looking at houses, but I loved people more. So, I quit selling real estate, and even though I was past fifty years old, I went back to Liberty University to earn a baccalaureate degree in counseling. (I originally went to college to get a bachelor, not a bachelor's degree.) I never loved studying. As a matter of fact, I hated studying. But when I returned to college, I found out that I had a great desire to improve my spiritual gift. Wanting to use my spiritual gift motivated me, drove me, made me overcome barriers in my life. I had quit college as soon as I got married; now, in order to sharpen my spiritual gift, I put myself through two years of "academic agony," receiving my B.S. degree in 1985. Then I worked in our church's counseling department, which offers professional help to people who can't pay a psychologist or psychiatrist.

Elmer again stepped in to upgrade my life. As dean of the School of Religion, he enrolled me in an introductory course he was teaching for those working on an M.A. in counseling. It was our way of being together on an evening when he had to be away from home, even though he was teaching and I was a student. But we did opt out for coffee after each class. Next, when Liberty University invited counseling authorities to teach, I enrolled in a course with a representative from the well-respected Minirth-Meier Clinic, and later took a course from Dr. Gary Collins, another respected Christian counselor. Before long, I had accumulated fifteen hours toward my M.A. degree, something I had adamantly said I would never do. But Elmer reasoned, "You're halfway to the M.A. Why don't you pay the price and finish?"

I did.

Eventually, God opened the door for me to become director of Family Life Services, the state-licensed adoption agency of our church. Attached to the agency is the Liberty Godparent Home, where single pregnant girls live free of charge until they deliver their babies. I counseled with young pregnant mothers and adoptive families, plus worked with the state licensing agency. I was supremely happy because I was doing the job for which God had gifted me. I'll always be grateful for that Sunday school lesson that turned my life around.

Every woman who serves the Lord serves Him differently. Why? Every woman has different spiritual gifts. Every woman has a different personality, and her personality influences her gift. Every woman comes from a different background, and her background influences the development of her gift. Every woman comes from a different family that influences its daughters differently. And every woman has a different temperament acquired from both birth and environment. Because God doesn't want His people to be carbon copies of one another, each woman has a different role in life, a different task to accomplish, and different giftedness to accomplish all the tasks God has given her to do. Because of this, God is glorified in the uniqueness of each of His servants. The fact that we are different is nowhere more taught than in the following passage,

"Having then gifts differing according to the grace that is given to us . . ." (Rom. 12:6).

Women—like men—serve the Lord according to the giftedness God has given them. The spiritual gifts given to women are no different than the spiritual gifts given to men. Since spiritual gifts are given to all believers, men and women alike receive them. God didn't designate certain gifts just for men, nor for women; therefore, we assume that women—like men—serve the Lord according to the same giftedness.

However, women serve the Lord differently than men. It's not that they try to be different; they *are* different.

Also, women were not designed to serve just women, and men were not designed to serve just men; God gave spiritual gifts to His children, and both women and men receive their gifts to serve each other. However, since a woman is not a man, a woman will exercise her spiritual giftedness with different feeling and flair than will a man. As an illustration, both men and women have the spiritual gift of teaching; however, when men teach, they tend to be more analytical and data-driven. Of course women are interested in analysis and data, but they tend to be driven more by heart and passion. The end result is that people learn the grace of God and grow in Jesus Christ through the gift of teaching. So, when men and women teach, people grow in grace and become like Jesus Christ. Remember, when men and women exercise the same gift, they tend to do it differently . . . according to their nature.

A gift doesn't always come wrapped in pretty paper, tied with silky ribbon and fluffy bows. Whatever the package, we try to give meaningful gifts—gifts we would enjoy receiving ourselves, or gifts to add to a hobby or collection. When purchasing a gift for someone, we remember a favorite color, fragrance, or taste preference. Our pleasure in giving is heightened by the way a gift is received with squeals of delight and expressions of gratitude.

Our God does not put a group of "grab bags" in a basket for us to "take one by chance." The gift God gives is uniquely designed to fit our individual personalities.

God is a loving Father who delights in giving gifts to His children. They are perfect gifts to extend our ministry. His gifts perfectly match

our personalities. Like a giver of gifts is pleased when a present she gives
is the perfect gift for an occasion, God is glorified when our gifts carry
out His will perfectly.

Women tend to be more concerned with what their spiritual giftedness does *to* them, whereas men may be more concerned with what their spiritual giftedness does *through* them. As an example, in the parable of the talents, the owner of the field gave to the first servant five talents, to the second servant three talents, and to the last servant one talent. Most sermons feature what the servants did with the talents, because most sermons are preached by men; however, when I (Ruth) read the parable of the talents, I am concerned with what the talents did to the servants who received them. Of course, the one who received five talents must have felt a special relationship to the Master. If the Lord gave me five talents, I would feel that the Lord loves me, trusts me, and wants to grow me into being a better servant. And of course, the servant with five talents brought back five more. That servant became a better servant because of the relationship. When you discover the talents the Master has given you, I want you to feel a special relationship to the Lord.

When this book talks about spiritual giftedness, my first concern is what will the gift do to the giftee, i.e., the person receiving the gift? If God gives to a certain woman the gift of evangelism, I believe three things apply to her. First, God has a special love to use her to win others to Himself. Second, God trusts her and therefore gives her opportunities to win others to Christ. And finally, God wants to grow her as she shares her faith with others.

We believe that every believer has every gift. That means every man and woman has the seed potential of every gift. It means that you—the reader—have every gift that God bestows upon His believers. So you shouldn't be saying, "I don't have the gift of evangelism or soul-winning." We believe every woman should be able to influence others to Christ. But at the same time, some women are more effective in sharing their faith than others. Some women have a strong gift of evangelism, while other women have a weak gift of evangelism. Therefore, as you read this book, try to determine the strength of your various gifts, and don't accept what you are as a final copy. God is not through with you yet. You can grow every gift to become a greater servant for God.

THE NINE TASK GIFTS

Evangelism: getting others to make a decision for salvation.

Helps: helping others by serving them.

Teaching: getting others to learn and grow.

Exhortation: motivating others to practical Christianity.

Giving: furthering God's will by providing for needs of others.

Administration: managing people, money, resources, and time.

Mercy-showing: supporting others through problems.

Prophecy: defending justice and the honor of God.

Shepherding: leading individuals and groups for Christ.

This book talks about nine gifts, and we believe that every person has at least a little bit of all nine gifts. Most of you will be strong in at least three areas, perhaps more. You can grow the areas where you are weak, "fan the flame of your giftedness" (2 Tim. 1:6, author's translation). At the same time, you have gifts that are strong. These are the gifts you ought to emphasize, so this book will help you determine your strengths and how to use them.

FINDING YOUR MINISTRY

There are many ways that women find their career and/or job. Sometimes, a woman just checks out the want ads in the local newspaper to see what is available, accepting a job for the best pay or the best working conditions. Sometimes a woman takes a job because she has to go into the family business—her father and mother were dentists, so she has to become a dentist too. Other times a woman accepts a job because of childhood dreams. Maybe as a young girl she played nurse and wanted to become a nurse; or she played school and dreamed of becoming a teacher. There are many women who only fulfill their childhood dreams in the workplace. Still a few others take a vocational preference inventory or some career track test to determine where they best fit in the workforce. All of these are good, but God always has a better way.

> A Christian woman should first discover her spiritual gifts (abilities), then find the best opportunity/place to use her spiritual giftedness.

This manuscript doesn't try to talk you into serving the Lord by painting a rosy picture of what you can do for God, nor does it try to give you a guilt trip by playing on your negative motivations to get you to serve God. Rather, this book helps you find your spiritual giftedness so you will know where you will perform best in the church—or wherever God leads you. The bottom line is, if you are serving God according to your spiritual giftedness, you can have a fruitful life of ministry, and it will be a lot more fun.

WHAT HAPPENS WHEN YOU USE YOUR SPIRITUAL GIFT?

You are fruitful.
You are blessed of God.
You are fulfilled.
You are motivated.
You are happy.

When you use your spiritual gifts in ministry, you will find satisfaction and fulfillment not previously experienced in other places. The opportunity of ministering in a children's class reaches out to you. If you have the gift of teaching, that opportunity can make you fruitful and satisfied, and God can use you better than if you were trying to do ministry for which you were not gifted.

We knew a woman in a church we attended years ago who had become the leader of the church choir. She usually put herself in to sing solos, accompanied by the choir. The problem was, she didn't have a strong voice, and she didn't always hit the right notes. We could see people in the congregation wince when she went flat on a high note. But there was a problem. Because it was a small church and everyone tried to treat others as a Christian, no one told her she was ill-suited to sing. Maybe they were afraid of offending her, or, perhaps the real reason, they couldn't get someone else to lead the choir. As a result, her service to the Lord was counterproductive. She could have served the Lord more effectively in the nursery, where her great love for children and tireless care of little ones could be more effective.

We served a church where JoAnn Moody, a high school girl, was often called to sing a solo. Sometimes when I (Elmer) was preaching and a song came to mind, I spontaneously asked JoAnn to come to the platform and sing the hymn. Without practice, she softly sang and we could feel the Spirit of God using her gentle giftedness. We could see tears in the eyes of people as her music touched hearts. JoAnn had a spiritual gift of exhortation manifested through music.

That should be your aim in life. That you find your gift as did JoAnn, and when you use it to the glory of God, hearts are touched, people grow in Christ, and as a result, knees are bowed to the Lord Jesus Christ.

I asked the server for sweetened tea and I assumed it would be sweetened the way my mother did it when I was young. When the tea was hot, she'd add sugar that would immediately dissolve in hot water. But this glass of tea was bitter, "Ugh-gh-gh," I responded to my wife because I didn't want to complain. "Look in the bottom," she said. "The sugar is in the bottom of the glass." When I asked for sweetened tea, the server just poured sugar in the bottom, but didn't stir it.

Spiritual gifts are like iced tea with sugar in the bottom of the glass. To get a little sweetness in your life, you've got to stir up your gifts. This is what Paul meant, "Stir up the gift of God" (2 Tim. 1:6).

Finding your spiritual gift should not be difficult. Check out spiritual gift inventories, ask a family member or close friend, survey your past experiences and what kind of Christian service makes you happy. What natural talent do you have that you could perfect with God's blessing? (These suggestions are explained fully in Chapter 10.)

This book is written with the prayer that you too will find your gift and serve God effectively.

Sincerely yours in Christ,

Ruth and Elmer Towns
From our home at the foot of the
Blue Ridge Mountains
Summer 2000

THE WOMAN AT THE WELL SHARED HER FAITH

THE SPIRITUAL GIFT OF EVANGELISM

Two ladies in church are as far apart in lifestyles and money as they are in pew locations. Betty, a plump woman who looks like a grandmother because of her prematurely graying hair and the shawl draped around her slumping shoulders, herds her six obedient children and husband into the second pew near the windows on the front left side. She reminds herself, "If the people of the church see us up front, they will pray for us."

Betty and her husband live in a large, old wooden home near downtown. Betty's husband's job in a grocery store doesn't pay enough to afford a better home in a better location. In spite of marginal finances, Betty's children have all the church advantages: camp, Christian private schooling, piano lessons, etc. Many of the women of the church have passed on to Betty the clothing that no longer fit their children or themselves. Betty has never been ashamed to be seen in a dress that was first worn by another lady of the church. Because Betty's children are polite to adults and obedient to their parents, men in the church contribute to a "Deacon's Fund," and out of that fund, Betty's children get these advantages.

Betty is a constant soul winner, talking to people about Jesus, trying to win them to salvation. She keeps tracts near the front door to give to every delivery person. She carries them in her purse to pass out to those waiting at the bus stop with her, and she gives them out to the salespeople when she shops.

Betty does everything possible to win unsaved people to Christ, including placing gospel tracts in Christmas cards, greeting cards, and in the envelopes when paying bills.

When the pastor gives a gospel invitation at the end of his sermon for people to come forward to receive Christ, Betty has gone to the counseling room to lead women to Christ. This is her greatest delight of the week.

Betty has a large prayer list of unsaved relatives for whom she prays. She has given out their names in church prayer meetings to get others to pray for them. No one in the church doubts Betty's sincerity as a personal evangelist.

Everyone thinks of Betty as a godly lady. Sitting in the front of the church keeps Betty in this focus. They admire her evangelistic activities, except when she confronts visitors to the church, asking them if they are saved. Some church members feel confrontation evangelism with visitors gives the wrong image of their congregation. They think her blunt approach might keep some visitors from returning again. Since it was discussed among several families, the church deacons took up the problem. While the deacons liked her evangelistic zeal and they admired her obedient children, they were not sure what to do about the problem. Rather than asking her not to meet the visitors, they arranged for Betty and her husband to duplicate audiotapes of the sermon immediately after the service so copies of the sermon could be included in a "hospitality package" that is handed to visitors as they leave church. This way, Betty feels she is helping to evangelize and the deacons feel their problem is solved. She is also thrilled to work side-by-side with her husband as they minister together.

Sitting at the back of the church under the balcony where she doesn't attract attention to herself, Marcy is the opposite of Betty. People who don't know Marcy don't think of her as spiritual because she is tall, slim, and stylish. Her manicured nails and the latest fashions, plus her Mercedes, the most expensive car in the church parking lot, with its vanity license plate, is the opposite of the image that Betty gives the congregation. Marcy's husband, a tax lawyer, is a deacon who quietly pays for Betty's six children to attend the Christian school in their church. That's because Marcy admires Betty's polite children and her constant attempts to win others to Christ.

Marcy has the spiritual gift of evangelism like Betty, but expresses it differently. In her devotions, Marcy intercedes for her neighbors to become believers, but she would never give their names out in prayer meeting because if the neighbors knew, they would be offended. When Marcy drops in to a neighbor's "mansion" for coffee, she doesn't preach to them, but she leaves a CD of contemporary Christian music, or a copy of one of the latest best-selling Christian books.

However, there are times when Marcy shares a verbal witness to her neighbors about Christ. When she invites them to her home, she feels this is her turf, so she has liberty to tell a friend how Jesus Christ is Master of her home and life.

Marcy was converted at the state university when a Bible study was held in her sorority house. She came to believe in Jesus as she asked questions about the Bible text they were studying that evening. The Campus Crusade for Christ workers didn't press Marcy to become a Christian; they just answered questions from the Bible. Finally, when all her questions were answered, Marcy concluded, "I have no reason to reject God!"

It was then and there that Marcy prayed to receive Christ. Now when Marcy shares coffee with her neighbors, she uses the same technique to win then to Christ. Marcy leads in a Bible study, answering their questions. Then Marcy asks, "Is there any reason for you to reject God?"

Marcy then leads them to pray to receive Christ, just as she did years ago in the sorority house. There are several families from the neighborhood that Marcy and her husband have led to Christ; these have all eventually become members of the church.

Because she keeps it quiet, most people in the church don't know about Marcy's evangelistic efforts, and if the congregation were asked who is the best soul winner in church, they would answer "Betty!" Even though Betty has led many people to Christ on the street corner and in stores, none of them have come into the church. The poor who live in Betty's neighborhood feel uncomfortable in her large brick church with its beautiful stained-glass windows. However, those Betty leads to Christ in the counseling room have become members. These two ladies both have the spiritual gift of evangelism, both share their faith, and both pray for unsaved people. However, they do it differently and they get different results, and God uses their gifts of evangelism according to their different circumstances and abilities.

WHAT IS THE GIFT OF EVANGELISM?

The woman with the gift of evangelism (1) has a consuming desire to see lost people believe in Jesus Christ, (2) will find ways to share her faith, (3) has discernment when the Holy Spirit is moving a person towards conversion, (4) has the ability to point people to Christ, and (5) has the skills to help them receive Christ.

UNDERSTANDING THE GIFT OF EVANGELISM

Where does the spiritual gift of evangelism come from? To answer this question look at the explanation of the nature of a spiritual gift in Scripture. "There are different kinds of abilities or gifts that come from the Holy Spirit. These gifts serve in different ways that come from the Lord Jesus. When we exercise these gifts, they produce different results, but it is God the Father who is working through these gifts" (1 Cor. 12:4–6, author's para-phrase). When you are given a spiritual gift, you are given a special ability by God to serve Him in a special way. It is God working through our abilities to accomplish His will. These verses tell us that God is the source of our giftedness and that each of us can serve Him in different ways and will have different outcomes. The woman with the gift of evangelism has a passion to share her faith, while the woman with the dominant gift of teaching wants to communicate Bible knowledge.

Do all have the same gifts? Not everyone teaches well, and not everyone can play the piano in church. God has given many different gifts to women in the body, each with their own special abilities. Some women sing soprano, others sing alto; we are made differently and we serve differently, each serving in her own special way. Peter tells us, "Each one should use whatever gift he has received to serve others, faithfully administering God's grace" (1 Peter 4:10 *NIV*). Not all women aggressively push their opinions on other women. Some don't share recipes or helpful house-cleaning hints, nor do they share much about their life. Therefore, they don't aggressively share their faith with others. They probably are not strongly gifted in evangelism. But even the ones who don't share Christ have an obligation to witness, because Jesus said, "You shall be witnesses" (Acts 1:8). The point is that all women are different, so all women will share their faith differently: some more aggressively than others, while some wait for the unsaved to ask them questions before they share their faith. But the point is all should share their faith.

You may not be a platform person (one who speaks in front of a group of people), but in your own quiet way you can tell others about Jesus—and that can be your ministry. Let God use you, according to the gifts He has given to you.

WEAKNESSES OR DANGERS OF THE GIFT OF EVANGELISM

The woman with this gift sometimes: (1) believes everyone should be an evangelist, (2) has a tendency to press for decisions before some are ready to receive Christ, (3) has a tendency to be confrontational, rather than relational, or (4) becomes result-oriented, rather than people-oriented.

Does every woman express the spiritual giftedness of evangelism the same way? Among men, some, such as Billy Graham, are great evangelists. Graham's daughter Ann Graham Lotz also has this gift. Some women witness to groups, while others witness to only one at a time. Some women are great soul winners and win many to Christ in their lifetime; while other women quietly witness for Jesus one at a time, and in their life have never had the privilege of praying with someone to receive Christ. However you express your spiritual gift of evangelism, use it as God has gifted you. "As everyone has received a gift, even so let them minister to one another" (1 Cor. 7:17, author's paraphrase).

How can women grow their gift of evangelism? Some women begin their Christian ministry by very quietly telling other people of Jesus, but they have never led anyone to Christ. Don't be discouraged if you don't see fruit at first. Your ability to share Christ can grow, and the results will increase as you learn how to do it. Paul told the Corinthians, "Eagerly desire the greater gifts" (1 Cor. 12:31 NIV). And in the same way, Paul writes to young Timothy, who needs encouragement, "For this reason I remind you to fan into flame the gift of God which is in you" (2 Tim. 1:6 NIV). This meant that Timothy had certain gifts that were hidden or not used. Paul was telling him to treat his gift like a smoldering fire. Timothy had to fan that small flame so it would become a larger fire. As we know, fire warms, cooks, and is a friendly companion. So fan the flame of your gift of evangelism so that God can use it to bring warmth to others in the body of Christ.

WATCHING FOR THE GIFT OF EVANGELISM IN YOUNG GIRLS

1. They want to invite friends to attend Sunday school with them.

2. They pray for their friends to know Jesus.

3. They freely talk about their faith to friends and relatives.

4. They are usually touched by evangelistic sermons.

5. They are outgoing in talking about their faith.

6. They actively minister to those around them and are aware of the spiritual condition of those they come in contact with on a daily basis.

7. They involve themselves with groups and programs that promote activities through evangelistic outreaches.

Why do we say all saved women have all spiritual gifts? First, because the motivation of the gifts is the Holy Spirit, and all saved women have the Holy Spirit living in their hearts, "His Spirit who dwells in you" (Rom. 8:11). Second, because God has given the general command to all believers to share their faith, "You shall be witnesses" (Acts 1:8). God would not give a woman the *responsibility* to share her faith without giving the *ability* to do it. And third, spiritual gifts are given like seeds to be planted, cultivated, and grown to maturity. Some women have a weak spiritual passion to evangelize. They are fearful and shy like the seed just planted. They need to grow their ability to share their faith. Other women have developed their ability to share their faith. They are like mature plants that produce fruit.

THE WOMAN AT THE WELL
John 4:4–42

An unnamed woman left her town of Sychar in the middle of the day to go to Jacob's Well because it was her task to fetch water for the house. Most women in Sychar went for water early in the morning and again at evening—when it was cool—where they enjoyed the company of other women and caught up on gossip. But this isolated woman came alone during the middle of the day, perhaps because she was ostracized by the other women of the village for her implied immorality. She had been married five times, and was now living with a man and not married to him. Since the Samaritan religion condemned such practices, this woman probably felt criticism from other women and came to the well by herself. Arriving at the well, she was startled by a Jewish man sitting on a bench who asked her a very simple question, "Will you give me something to drink?"

April was usually hot, the temperature reaching 90-100 degrees during the last days of the month. Because Jesus had already walked a long distance and was hot and thirsty, He asked for a drink of water.

The woman was surprised because the Jews didn't have anything to do with Samaritans, compounded by the fact that men looked down on women, and a Jewish man would not be caught dead talking to a Samaritan woman. She responded, "Why are you asking me for a drink?"

Jesus didn't directly answer her question, but He captured her attention, "But if you knew who I am, and the gift of God, you would ask Me for water, and I would give you living water."

"But you don't have a rope or bucket," the woman responded. "The well is very deep, there is no way for you to draw water for me."

At first the woman was concerned with the natural obstacles of getting water out of the deep well, until she realized Jesus had promised her "living water." She turned her thoughts to an obvious religious controversy.

"Do you think that You are greater than our forefather Jacob who dug this well? How can you offer water that is better than what Jacob gave to his family and flocks?"

"You will become thirsty after drinking this water," Jesus answered, "but the water I will give to you will take away all your thirst. You won't have to draw water again, because my water will be an artesian well of water that will spring up within you, giving you eternal life."

"Please," the woman begged, "give me living water so that I will never be thirsty again. I won't have to come to this well and fetch water again."

Jesus knew the woman because He was God. He knew that her sin would have to be revealed before she would seek salvation. So Jesus told her, "Go call your husband."

"I don't have a husband," the woman answered him.

"You're right." Jesus answered. "You don't have a husband now, but you have had five husbands and now you're not married to the man you're living with."

The woman was shocked at this revelation, "You must be a prophet," she answered. The woman wanted to argue, "So tell me, should I worship in Jerusalem where You say is the only place, or can I worship on Mount Gerizim where Samaritans worship?"

"Neither." Jesus answered her. "The time is coming when people will no longer worship in Jerusalem or on this mountain." In this statement Jesus pointed her to a greater truth. "The time is coming when true worshipers will worship the Father in spirit and in truth." Jesus continued to explain, "God is Spirit and they who worship Him must worship Him in spirit and in truth."

The woman needed convincing. She knew the Messiah would be greater than the prophets, so she said, "I know that Messiah will come—the One called Christ—He will explain the right religion to us when He comes."

"I am the Messiah," Jesus said to her.

At this moment the disciples arrived from town with food for Jesus. They were astonished that He was talking with a woman—a fallen woman—even though they were talking out in the open where all could see them. The woman left her water jar by the well and went running back into town, telling everyone she met, "Come and see a man who told me everything that I ever did! Can this be the Messiah?"

How did the woman evidence the gift of evangelism? When a woman has the gift of evangelism, she doesn't have to force herself to tell other people about her conversion—most can see it. She doesn't have to force herself to tell other people what changed her. She naturally tells others about what happened to her. Telling others about Jesus is as natural as telling others about a diet or about a new way of cooking that made her family happy. Because women like to share, they tell others about Jesus Christ who has changed their life. The woman who met Jesus at the well went everywhere saying, "Come, see a Man who told me all things that ever I did. Could this be the Christ?" (John 4:29).

What is another evidence that the woman had the gift of evangelism? There is an old saying, "What's in the well, comes up in the bucket." And we know "what's in the heart comes out of the mouth." So it's only natural that this woman, whose life was changed by Jesus, wanted other people to have the same experience. But she did more than share her experience; she convinced others of what she was saying. She convinced others to believe in Jesus as she did. "Many of the Samaritans of that city believed in Him because of the word of the woman" (John 4:39).

What is the motivation of the person with the gift of evangelism? The woman at the well met Jesus Christ, had her questions answered, and knew in her heart that He was the Messiah. She did not go off to find a lonely spot to pray, nor did she go into the harvest fields about her to gather grain, nor did she continue with her task of fetching water. She went back to the men of the city—because men knew her better than women—and told them about Jesus. A woman with the gift of evangelism looks for ways to share her faith. "The woman then left her waterpot, went her way into the city, and said to the men" (John 4:28).

What is the passion of the woman with the gift of evangelism? The woman had a new gift of evangelism that enabled her to live outside of herself. This woman who had gone through five marriages lived a self-centered life, and probably could not keep a husband because she was more interested in herself than the husband. But when she met Jesus, she lost her self-centered interest and went to tell others about Jesus.

She didn't tell them about herself—time was too short. She didn't use her wisdom or persuasive ability to motivate others. All she could do was testify of Jesus. "Many of the Samaritans . . . believed in Him because of the word of the woman who testified, 'He told me all that I ever did'" (John 4:39).

Too many women try to "win souls" with a special plan such as *The Four Spiritual Laws* or *The Roman Road of Salvation* (see Practical Take-aways). While plans are good to follow and you will probably want to use them in sharing your faith, remember, it is not a special formula to present the gospel that will get others saved. You will win others to Christ with your sincerity and passion.

Some women try to win their friends with persuasive arguments, debates, or by quoting the right verse at the right time. When the cult members come to the front door—usually in pairs—some women try to answer all their questions and "debate" these people into salvation. We're not saying you shouldn't do this; we're saying you don't *have* to debate them. There are better ways to share your faith.

Some women try to evangelize by pointing out the sins of the person they are trying to win to Jesus. Their whole contention is to get the person under conviction of sin so they will feel "lost" and become a Christian.

However, let us learn from the woman at the well. She had passion—a deep desire—to tell others what Jesus did for her. Her passion motivated her simply to share her testimony. She carried an empty vessel to the well to get some water, but it was the vessel of her life that was filled with the living water of Jesus. As she ran back into town, the living water spilled to others. Her passion made her share who Jesus was and what He had done for her. Today, we call this sharing your testimony with an unsaved person.

WHAT YOUR TESTIMONY SHOULD INCLUDE

1. What you were before conversion.
2. How you received Christ.
3. What happened at your conversion.
4. What Christ means to you now.

What is the main issue when a woman exercises her gift of evangelism? When the woman first met Jesus, she wanted to argue with Him. First, she argued that He did not have the physical bucket or rope. Second, she tried to argue about the right place to worship God. Jesus did not argue with her; He simply told her who He was. What changed her life? Jesus Christ! What convinced the people of the city? They came to know Jesus as she did. "Then they said to the woman, 'Now we believe because we have heard him ourselves, not just because of what you told us. He is indeed the Savior of the world'" (John 4:42 TLB). The main issue of evangelism is Jesus.

PRACTICAL TAKE-AWAYS

The following questions were written for group discussion with a Sunday school class or Bible study. These questions are written in the first person to help you personalize your answers and apply them to your life.

1. *Can I actually lead someone to pray to receive Christ?* Yes! You don't have to be in full-time ministry to point other people to Jesus. The Bible is filled with illustrations of average people who shared their faith with others. This chapter gives the illustration of the woman at the well bringing faith to the men of her village. Philip was the only person in the Bible who was called an evangelist (Acts 21:8), yet he originally was a layperson who was elevated to be a deacon (Acts 6:5). Finally, he became an evangelist. You don't have to be an evangelist to tell other people about Jesus. You don't have to be on the church staff, or elected to a church office; all you have to be is a believer who shares her faith with others.

STEPS TO LEADING A PERSON TO CHRIST

Share your faith with them.

Tell them what Christ has done for you.

Explain how you actually accepted Christ.

Ask them if they want Christ to do for them what He has done for you.

Lead in prayer and let them pray with you.

2. *Will I have to speak in public?* You don't have to be a public speaker to point others to Jesus Christ. You can invite a friend over for brunch to tell her what Jesus has done for you. This can be a planned moment to share your testimony, or it can be spontaneous at a coffee break. On other occasions, when it naturally comes up in a conversation, tell others what Jesus has done for you. Your gift of evangelism can be personally, intimately, and quietly done.

3. *Should I always try to give a special presentation of the gospel?* Some people have taken an evangelism class at church and learned *The Roman Road of Salvation* to lead people to Christ. It is called the Roman Road because all four verses are found in the book of Romans. *The Roman Road of Salvation* is an effective plan. Both of us—Ruth and Elmer—have these verses underlined in our Bibles so that when someone wants to know about salvation, we can show them these verses.

The Four Spiritual Laws is also a wonderful means of learning how to share Jesus Christ. It begins with a positive approach of telling people of God's love for them. *The Four Spiritual Laws* comes from Campus Crusade for Christ and is a beautiful formula to help lead an unsaved person to Jesus Christ.

THE ROMAN ROAD OF SALVATION

Human Need	Romans 3:23
Sin's Penalty	Romans 6:23
God's Provision	Romans 5:8
The Person's Response	Romans 10:9

THE FOUR SPIRITUAL LAWS

1. God loves you and has a wonderful plan for your life.

2. Man is sinful and separate from God; thus, he cannot know and experience God's plan for his life.

3. Jesus Christ is God's only provision for man's sin. Through Him, you can know and experience God's love and plan for your life.

4. We must individually receive Him as Savior and Lord. Then we can know and experience God's love and plan for our lives.

Evangelism Explosion is another popular approach used to lead people to Christ that was first suggested by D. James Kennedy. It begins with a question to get people thinking about their spiritual condition.

EVANGELISM EXPLOSION

1. Have you come to a place in your spiritual life where you can say for certain that if you were to die today you would go to Heaven?

2. Suppose that you were to die tonight and stand before God and He were to say to you, "Why should I let you into My Heaven?" What would you say?[1]

Actually, you don't need to use any specific approach. Remember the Bible story explained earlier in this chapter? The woman left the well, and "went her way into the city . . . to the men" (John 4:28). She didn't have time to learn a formula. After she met Jesus, she simply told others what Jesus did for her. Some women will be more comfortable using a formula, others will be more spontaneous. God will use both approaches. But remember, just as a person can't give the measles if she doesn't have the measles; so a person can't give the joy of Jesus to others if she has not found inner peace in Him.

4. *How should I answer someone who wants to argue?* At first the woman at the well wanted to argue with Jesus about where to worship, but Jesus refused to argue with her. He simply pointed her to the truth and told her who He was. Follow the example of Jesus. Some might argue with you about their ideas or their religion. Note two things! First, you can't argue lost people into the kingdom, but you can love them to Christ. While arguing can remove a barrier that may block a lost person from salvation, arguing doesn't get anyone saved. Second, you don't need to argue. That's not God's plan for evangelism. All you need to do is to tell others about Jesus and what He means to you.

5. *Should I push for results?* You are not responsible for results, you are only required to be a faithful witness for Christ. You plant the seed, and God will give growth and the fruit. All you can do is point people to Jesus. The woman gave a very simple invitation, "Come, see a Man . . ." (John 4:29). Any woman who points others to Jesus can be a witness.

6. *Should I wait to evangelize until my ability gets stronger?* There are some women who are reluctant to share their faith, wrongly thinking, "I don't have the gift of evangelism." Other women use the excuse, "I'm gifted in another area." Don't try to hide behind these excuses, thinking you have another dominant gift, or you don't have the gift of evangelism. Many people will have spiritual gifts that are stronger than their gift of evangelism, but that is no excuse why they should not share their faith. John Wesley advised young believers to use what faith they had and it would grow stronger. If you use your weak gift of evangelism, it will grow stronger.

7. *Where should I begin?* Every person has different strengths in different areas. Look at all your spiritual gifts. Determine the strongest and the weakest. How your spiritual gifts interrelate is called your *gift mix*. Learn your unique gift mix. Know where you are weak, but don't let that get you discouraged. Do what you are best at, and get strength to tackle your weaknesses from doing what you do best.

> Know your giftedness.
>
> Know your strength.
>
> Do what you do best.
>
> Be faithful in small abilities.

8. *How can I grow my spiritual gift of evangelism?* Everyone has some gift of evangelism, so begin with your responsibility and ability. Begin where you are and plan to become better in sharing your faith with other people. Don't hide behind the excuse, "I'm weak in evangelism." When given the opportunity, tell others about Jesus Christ. There are several ways to grow your gift: (1) pray and ask God to increase your courage and knowledge of people; (2) study all gifts (in this book) and you will become stronger in all areas of ministry; (3) take the Spiritual Gift Questionnaire at the back of this book to determine your strongest gifts (then be realistic about your gift of evangelism); (4) plan and seek ways to begin witnessing and begin in a non-confrontational way; (5) make friends with someone with the intent of sharing Jesus with them; (6) do intentional things such as sharing Christian books, cassette messages, praise music, practical magazine articles on faith, and other things that will open up opportunities to share Jesus; (7) after praying for a person, do intentional things to win that person to yourself; such as taking her baked goods, offering to baby-sit, or some other act of kindness; (8) invite her to church or a Christian meeting with you; and (9) ask her to attend your church's function for ladies.

STEPS TO WIN SOMEONE TO CHRIST

1. Win the person to yourself.
2. Win the person to your church.
3. Win the person to Christ.

THREE-STEP BIBLE STUDY

Step One, read the questions to get you thinking about God's name.

Step Two, analyze the verses with each question to see what the Bible says about the question.

Step Three, write your answers in the space provided.

1. **What is the condition of others that would motivate you to share your faith with them?**

   "For the wages of sin is death, but the gift of God is eternal life in Christ Jesus our Lord"
   (Rom. 6:23).

   _____

   _____

   _____

2. **What will happen to your friends and relatives if they don't accept Jesus as Savior?**

   "For the wages of sin is death, but the gift of God is eternal life in Christ Jesus our Lord"
   (Rom. 6:23).

   _____

   _____

   _____

3. **What is the greatest news you have to share with others?**

   "But God demonstrates His own love toward us, in that while we were still sinners, Christ died for us" (Rom. 5:8).

   _____

   _____

   _____

4. **What must others do to become a Christian?**

   ". . . that if you confess with your mouth the Lord Jesus and believe in your heart that God has raised Him from the dead, you will be saved" (Rom. 10:9).

   _____

   _____

   _____

5. **What will happen to a person if he or she prays to receive Christ?**

   "But as many as received Him, to them He gave the right to become children of God, to those who believe in His name" (John 1:12).

   _____

   _____

   _____

6. **What happens after a person prays to become a Christian?**

   "Therefore, if anyone is in Christ, he is a new creation; old things have passed away; behold, all things have become new" (2 Cor. 5:17).

   _____

   _____

   _____

   _____

7. **The Bible describes evangelism as "winning souls." What does this picture mean to you?**

   "The fruit of the righteous is a tree of life, And he that winneth souls is wise" (Prov. 11:30).

   _____

   _____

   _____

   _____

YOUR TIME TO PRAY

Add the following requests to your daily prayer list. As you pray about developing the gift of evangelism, you will find several things happening in your life: (1) Prayer gives you a desire to use your gift; (2) prayer gives you wisdom to use your gift (James 1:5); (3) prayer influences the lives of those you touch in ministry; (4) God answers by growing your gift; and (5) you grow to maturity in Christ and become more effective in use of all gifts.

1. Pray for God to help you see the spiritual condition of those around you, "But when He [Jesus] saw the multitudes, He was moved with compassion for them, because they were weary and scattered, like sheep having no shepherd" (Matt. 9:36). *Lord, open my eyes to see my friends and relatives as You see them.*

2. Confess your fears, and wrong ideas about witnessing for Christ. Ask God to forgive you, *"If we confess our sins, He is faithful and just to forgive us our sins and to cleanse us from all unrighteousness (1 John 1:9).* Now, determine to share your faith with others. *Lord, I've been scared to witness and I've claimed that witnessing was not my responsibility; I'm sorry for being disobedient. Help me witness to others.*

3. Pray that you grow in love for others. "Jesus said to him, 'You shall love the LORD your God with all your heart, with all your soul, and with all your mind.' This is the first and great commandment. And the second is like it: You shall love your neighbor as yourself'" (Matt. 22:37–39). *Lord, I love You, but I don't love You enough; help me to grow in my love for You and for others.*

4. Make a prayer list of unsaved relatives, friends, and business acquaintances. Begin asking God to help you reach everyone on that list for Christ. *Lord, I have many unsaved friends and relatives; help me be a good witness to them.*

5. Your personal prayer list.

_____

_____

_____

_____

_____

JOURNALING AND MEDITATION

As you study this workbook, think about the things you are learning by writing them down. You will clarify your thoughts as you express them in words. Journaling turns feelings into acts and helps you understand what's happening internally. Actually, your journal—like a diary—is like a mirror that helps you look into your soul.

1. Write out any experiences when you shared your faith with another person. First, write what you actually did and said. Then list the positive results of your witnessing experience. If there were negative things—perhaps just weaknesses—write these out also.

2. Look within yourself to face the reasons you don't share your faith. Sometimes you don't witness because you are afraid of embarrassment or threats, or you don't want others to know how little you know about the Bible and your faith. Write these out. Facing them on paper may help you overcome your reluctance to witness. By writing these things in your journal, you may actually help strengthen your gift of evangelism.

3. What journaling can look like:

Day One

When I was little I went shopping with my mother or to a circus with my dad. My excitement was always clouded by the fear that somehow in the crowd, I would get lost.

As I grew older, I would not admit being lost or unable to find my way. I don't like the feeling of being lost. I don't want someone to say, "Oh, that poor little girl is lost. Let's help her find her mommy."

Why is it then that I'm not as concerned as I should be about someone who is eternally lost?

"Lord, lay some soul upon my heart and love that soul through me, and may I humbly do my part to win that soul for thee." (Ruth)

Day Two

I was so upset! Somehow I had misplaced or completely lost a pair of tiny diamond earrings my husband gave me. I got down on my hands and knees and covered every inch of carpet in the bedroom. I prayed. I cried. I was angry at myself for being careless.

Before climbing into bed one night, I stepped on something hard and sharp: one diamond earring! As I quickly searched the floor, I yelled out loud when the lost was found.

Diamonds are costly but souls are precious. I'm reminded that the angels rejoice when one soul is saved . . . when one lost sheep is found.

4. Now your turn to journal:

_____

_____

_____

_____

_____

_____

_____

_____

_____

_____

_____

_____

_____

_____

_____

_____

_____

_____

[1] D. James Kennedy, *Evangelism Explosion* (Wheaton, Ill. Tyndale House Publishers, 1977), 51.

PHOEBE HELPED PAUL'S MINISTRY

THE SPIRITUAL GIFT OF HELPS

Two women in the same local church have the spiritual gift of helps and both use their gifts in service at their church, yet they use their gifts of helps differently; each helps people in her own unique way. The first, Abigail, has a full-time job using her gifts, while the second, "Grandma," uses her gifts as a layperson in the church. Abigail has been secretary in the small-town church for six pastors for more than two-and-a-half decades. She's seen young, aggressive pastors come only to be called to larger churches in the city. She's seen older pastors come in their retirement years only to die or move on to a nursing home. Through the good pastors and weak ones—for twenty-six years—Abigail has been the glue that has kept the church together.

Now, Abigail is a grandmother. Her three children grew up in the church and moved away to the city, so she has more time than ever to give to church activities. Abigail looks after the congregation as though the church members were her children and grandchildren.

Beyond secretarial duties, she runs by the hospital to deliver a church bulletin or some flowers out of her garden. Three of the single, working mothers in church didn't know what to do with their small children after school. So, Abigail keeps an eye on them while they do their homework in the church parlor until their moms get off work. The church secretary has used her skills to critique some of their homework, and even to help.

Abigail can't do enough for the church or the members. She loves her job. On Sunday morning she fills in if a teacher doesn't show up. She will answer more questions about the week's schedule than the pastor or chairman of the board, because everyone realizes Abigail knows everything that's going on.

After surgery two years ago, Abigail was placed on leave from her job for a month to recuperate. She then took a four-week vacation to visit her grandchildren. While she was gone, a deacon's wife who was a retired secretary filled in for the six weeks. The fill-in secretary would not look after the children of the single moms after school, nor did she do all the little things that Abigail did. The deacon's wife was a professional secretary with outstanding skills—not a chauffeur, errand girl, coffee-maker, message-taker, counselor, and fill-in "Girl Friday."

Everyone was thrilled when Abigail returned.

Abigail sees herself as a secretary and a minister for Christ, doing whatever she can to help people and ultimately help the church. She knows her spiritual gift is *helps*, and she gets fulfillment in life doing what God has gifted her to do.

The second woman in the church is "Grandma," the name everyone in the church uses. They call her "Grandma" because her children called her that in front of her grandchildren. Even from the pulpit, the pastor referred to her as "Grandma," and it was more than a title of age; it was a term of endearment. Everybody loves Grandma because of what she does for everyone.

Because Grandma always went straight to the church nursery when she came to church, the younger mothers got together to take their turn watching the babies, because they felt Grandma needed to be in worship sometimes, just like everyone else. Every time there was a church supper, Grandma showed up first, sprucing up the kitchen, getting it ready for the covered dishes. After everything was over, she was the last one to leave, drying a dish or sweeping a floor. Just before leaving, she'd look around the kitchen, taking pride in its cleanliness, just as she took pride in her spotless kitchen at home.

Grandma grew up on a farm and has been growing a vegetable garden every year since she got married. During the Depression when finances were tight, she fed her family vegetables. During World War II, hers was the largest victory garden in the neighborhood. Because she would rather have fresh vegetables than what she called "store bought," she continued feeding her children and grandchildren from her garden. Even now, she grows enough for all her family, plus anyone in the church needing anything. When tomatoes are ripe, Grandma brings several plastic bags of delicious ruby red tomatoes to distribute among the different families in the church. No one is offended to carry his bags of tomatoes away from the church, except the few casual visitors who didn't get any. And if Grandma knew that they wanted some, she would have provided for them too.

After her husband died, Grandma had three extra bedrooms in the large old house. She was always the first to volunteer to keep missionaries coming through town on their visit to the churches. And if they could stay three or four days before they traveled on to the next church, Grandma delighted in feeding them, washing and ironing their clothes, and patching anything that needed mending.

Although she loved her husband dearly, she has never had a lot of lonely hours to sit around and miss him. She stays busy baby-sitting the grandkids, or helping them with homework. She's taught every grandchild how to open a checking account, balance his or her checkbook, and pay his or her bills. Grandma is even pretty good at filling out income tax forms for her grandchildren and the other elderly people in the neighborhood.

When someone mentioned to Grandma that she had the gift of helps or serving, she didn't know how to respond. Grandma was never taught the doctrine of spiritual gifts and has never thought about using her spiritual gifts. She doesn't even know about her *gift mix*. Grandma's response was, "I just do what I like to do, and I do what I do best."

UNDERSTANDING THE GIFT OF HELPS

The woman with the spiritual gift of helps or ministry loves to perform service-oriented work for Christ, as do Abigail and Grandma. She enjoys doing routine tasks that are called *mundane* by others, but she does them quietly without public attention. She knows that Jesus was a servant-leader and she follows His example.

How important is the gift of helps? While this gift is not mentioned first in order of importance, the gift is all-important to the one who possesses it. "And God has appointed these in the church: first apostles, second prophets, third teachers, after that . . . helps" (1 Cor. 12:28). If you have the gift of serving or helps, your tasks will be as important as you make them. The list of God is not quantitative in importance, only qualitative.

WHAT IS THE GIFT OF HELPS?

The woman with the gift of helps has the ability (1) to serve God in task-oriented gifts, (2) to minister to the physical and spiritual needs of others, (3) to serve without fanfare, (4) to work for immediate goals, and (5) to get satisfaction out of completing tasks.

What is the focus of the spiritual gift of helps? Paul tells us, "Having then gifts differing according to the grace that is given to us . . . if . . . ministry, let us use it in our ministering" (Rom. 12:6, 7). In this verse, the gift of helps is called ministry. If you have the gift of ministering to others or serving others, you will look for a place to use it. The NIV uses a different term to explain the same spiritual gift, "If it is serving, let him [her] serve" (Rom. 12:7). The Living Bible gives the focus of this gift, "If your gift is that of serving others, serve them well" (Rom. 12:7). The focus is helping others for the glory of God.

Should every woman serve? All Christian women have all gifts—at least they have some of each gift to some degree. So no matter who you are, you have some giftedness in serving other people. Remember, Paul commanded all, "Serve one another" (Gal. 5:13). Because God is just, when He gave all the responsibility to serve, He also gave His people the ability to carry out the command. Also, since all believers have the Holy Spirit, and He is sent as our Comforter, i.e., Helper, then it means the Holy Spirit would naturally use us to help others.

WATCHING FOR THE GIFT OF HELPS IN YOUNG GIRLS

1. They like to help with the preparation of meals or setting the table, and they do it well.
2. They automatically help an older sister or aunt care for the small needs of her baby, and they relieve the mother of some responsibility.
3. They are office helpers or assist their teachers at school.
4. They usually keep their rooms tidy and they organize their clothes.
5. They make good baby-sitters.
6. They look after the needs of younger brothers or sisters.
7. They are helpful to their friends.

Is serving the dominant gift of all women? Some may have the dominant gift of teaching, and others are evangelists, but perhaps your dominant gift is helping. If so, don't expect someone without this dominant gift to serve the way you do. Allow every woman to serve from her strength. Some serve by teaching or by evangelizing while you serve by performing routine tasks.

When Paul said, "Each . . . has his [her] own gift" (1 Cor. 7:7), he indicated we have an identifying gift. Paul reminds us of some of these identifying gifts. "First apostles, second prophets, third teachers" (1 Cor. 12:28). This means some were known by their gift, i.e., they had a dominant gift. The one person we know who had the gift of serving was Phoebe, because Paul said, "Phoebe . . . who is a servant of the church" (Rom. 16:1). Phoebe was a helper and she helped people by serving them.

WHAT THE GIFT OF HELPS DOES:

Women wash dishes, clean the sanctuary, are Sunday school secretaries and class hostesses, welcome new people, type bulletins, answer phones, and serve meals at church suppers. Those with the gift of helps mop floors, direct traffic, baby-sit, phone absentees, fold bulletins, replace burned-out lights, rake leaves, put up Christmas decorations, and distribute flyers.

How is the gift of serving expressed? Some women are great in relationships, so they serve in areas of hospitality, meeting people and helping people feel comfortable in the church. The next woman is good with her hands, so she serves in the kitchen or church office. Another loves to grow things at home, so she uses her gift of serving by looking after the flower beds of the church. Still another person serves through her creativity or artistic expression. She may work with decorations, clothes, flowers, or music.

PHOEBE THE HELPER

"I commend to you Phoebe our sister, who is a servant of the church in Cenchrea, that you may receive her in the Lord in a manner worthy of the saints, and assist her in whatever business she has need of you; for indeed she has been a helper of many and of myself also"
(Rom. 16:1, 2).

Very little is said about Phoebe, a woman with the spiritual gift of helps; she's mentioned in only one passage of Scripture. She was serving in the church of Cenchrea, a little town on the eastern shore of the harbor of Corinth in Greece, when Paul arrived there on his third journey. In a single sentence, Paul says five things about her. She: (a) is a sister in Christ, (b) is a servant, (c) had a good track record ("she has been a helper of many and of myself also"), (d) is important ("assist her"), and (e) carried the epistle of Romans from Corinth after Paul wrote it to the church at Rome. Phoebe probably already had planned on taking this trip; otherwise Paul would have sent it by one of his traveling companions.

What does the word servant *mean?* Too often people think that a servant is like a slave, one who is owned and commanded to work for another person. A servant in the church is owned by Jesus Christ and serves Him. However, a biblical servant chooses to help or serve others because that is the way she serves Jesus Christ. God moved Paul to include a description of this woman to illustrate a female servant, who served the Lord by helping the church and Paul. Notice it says of Phoebe that as she helped others, she ministered to God.

When you have the spiritual giftedness of being a servant, you serve the church of Jesus Christ, which means you serve other believers who fellowship with you and serve with you. "Phoebe . . . a servant of the church" (Rom. 16:1).

What should be the attitude of the church toward those who serve it? Just because a woman is a servant doesn't mean she is a doormat or that her feelings should be ignored. We should have the same attitude toward those who serve the church as Paul wanted the Romans to have toward Phoebe, "That you may receive her in the Lord" (16:2). Paul reminds us that everyone should have the gift of serving—"serve one another" (Gal. 5:13); therefore, no person in the church is a "boss" to another. To put it another way, just as Jesus took a towel and basin to wash the feet of His disciples, we must symbolically wash the feet of everyone in our church by serving Him.

How does a woman with this gift serve others? More than just serving one another, we should assist each other in service, making everyone's tasks easier as we try to accomplish the goals of the church. Notice what Paul told the church to do about Phoebe, "Assist her in whatever business she has need of you" (Rom. 16:2). What Paul wanted the church to do for Phoebe is not unlike what Jesus said of us, "No longer do I call you servants . . . but I have called you friends" (John 15:15). Even though we all serve one another, our relationship to Jesus Christ makes us more than servants; we are His friends and members one of another.

How can the gift of serving be best used? Paul tells us, "She [Phoebe] has been a helper of many" (Rom. 16:2). By using our gift of serving a few in the church, we serve many. And when we serve the local body of Christ, we serve Jesus Himself.

A local church sometimes has difficulty when some are egocentric and prideful in their service. When a person must be the bride at every wedding and corpse at every funeral, that person disrupts the unity of the church. Unless everyone is willing to serve others, the church will never arrive at the unity expected by Jesus Christ.

Are any exempted from serving the church? Even though Paul knew that Phoebe was his helper, Paul understood the role of serving the church. He said at one place, "For though I am free from all men, I have made myself a servant to all" (1 Cor. 9:19). Because Paul was willing to serve everyone—and Paul is certainly important—then, by his example, we must all serve one another.

PRACTICAL TAKE-AWAYS

The following questions were written for group discussion with a Sunday school class or Bible study. These questions are written in the first person to help you personalize your answers and apply them to your life.

Some feel God is only interested in theoretical things like our doctrinal statement, sermon, or understanding biblical principles by which we live. However, God is practical and He has given practical people to the church who turn on the lights, clean the sanctuary, pass out bulletins, arrange flowers, and smooth relationships so people will live together in harmony.

1. *How can I know inwardly that I have the gift of serving*? Go deep within yourself to look at your desire. Ask yourself, "What do I like to do?" If you enjoy working with your hands, or doing tasks for others, you may be gifted in serving. A lady in our early morning prayer meeting at church has the gift of serving. She comes early to pick up any paper or pencils on the floor, or any items left in the prayer room. If it gets too hot or cold while we're praying, she's the one who gets up to adjust the thermostat. When someone leaves the door open, she's the one who gets up to close it. She makes sure there are no distractions while we are praying. She services the intercessors of the church so they may pray more effectively.

You can take a spiritual gift questionnaire to find out if you have the gift of helps. But most adults know what they like to do and what they are good at doing. Usually, what you enjoy doing for God and what you do well is the area where God has gifted you.

2. *What is an outward indication that I have the gift of helps?* When you see that a task needs to get done, and you see how to do it; this is another indication that you have the giftedness of service. When a woman with the gift of helps walks into the church kitchen that has been left in a mess by a high school group after a pizza party, she not only knows that someone ought to clean it up, she knows exactly how to proceed. Almost without thinking, she goes from task to task, and systematically finishes the job without frustration or bitterness toward the high school kids. Because she loves to serve, she cleans up the kitchen. Anyone else would probably want to chew out the kids because they broke the kitchen rules.

3. *What will I see if I have the gift of helps*? The woman with the giftedness of serving sees what the job looks likes when finished, even before she begins. In the previous paragraph, when the woman with the gift of helps went into the messy kitchen, she knew exactly where everything should go, and what a clean kitchen looks like, before she began. When she got finished, there was not a crumb on the counter or a dirty cloth in the sink; even the dishes were dried and placed in the cabinets. She probably took one last glance around the kitchen, just to make sure everything was in place.

4. *What will give me satisfaction if I have the gift of helps?* If you have the gift of helps, you'll get satisfaction out of a job well done. Remember the woman in the previous paragraph. She walks out of the kitchen feeling good about making the kitchen beautiful and serviceable again. She didn't have to force herself to clean the kitchen, it came naturally. A woman with the gift of helps identifies with a clean kitchen. The greatest satisfaction of a woman who has the spiritual gift of helping is her own fulfillment in doing the job well. She does not need someone to come by and tell her, "That looks great"; she knows what is good.

WEAKNESSES OR DANGERS OF THE GIFT OF HELPS

The woman with this gift may (1) be too practically-oriented to the exclusion of biblical orientation, (2) be insensitive to content ministries, (3) wrongly interpret spiritual desires that are not practical, (4) be prideful in a job well done, or (5) be critical of steps of faith that appear unpractical.

5. *How often will I repeat a task if I have the gift of helps?* And if it happens again—the teenagers have another pizza party—the woman with the gift of helps is willing to clean up the kitchen again . . . and again . . . and again. Those with the giftedness of serving others, do it gladly; they can do it many times because it is their nature. Serving others is what they want to do.

6. *When I serve other people, whom am I serving?* In one sense, you serve because of who you are. We had an aunt who always entered the house and went straight to the kitchen to help. The same thing happened when she went to church; she always went to the church kitchen and picked up a cloth to clean a counter or a towel to dry dishes. One time I heard another woman asking her why she always went straight for the kitchen.

"Because it's in me," she explained. "I like to help."

Ponder her answer carefully. Are you a person who helps others because it comes out of your inner self? Some women find the meaning of their life in doing tasks for other people.

Jesus said, "If I then, your Lord and Teacher, have washed your feet, you also ought to wash one another's feet. For I have given you an example, that you should do as I have done to you" (John 13:14, 15). In another place, He said, "Inasmuch as you did it to one of the least of these My brethren, you did it to Me" (Matt. 25:40). When we serve other people, we are serving Jesus Christ.

THREE-STEP BIBLE STUDY

Step One, read the questions to get you thinking about God's name.

Step Two, analyze the verses with each question to see what the Bible says about the question.

Step Three, write your answers in the space provided.

1. **What is the focus of the spiritual gift of service?**

   "Having then gifts differing according to the grace that is given to us . . . if . . . ministry, let us use it in our ministering" (Rom. 12:6, 7). "And God has appointed these in the church, first apostles, second prophets, third teachers, after that . . . helps" (1 Cor. 12:28).

   _____

   _____

   _____

2. **How did Phoebe serve the church?**

   "I commend to you Phoebe our sister, who is a servant of the church in Cenchrea, that you may receive her in the Lord in a manner worthy of the saints, and assist her in whatever business she has need of you; for indeed she has been a helper of many and of myself also" (Rom. 16:1–2).

   _____

   _____

   _____

3. What was Phoebe's title? Do you like this title?

"Phoebe . . . a servant of the church" (Rom. 16:1).

_____

_____

_____

4. What should be our *attitude* to those who serve the church?

*"That you may receive her in the Lord" (Rom. 16:2). "Through love serve one another"
(Gal. 5:13).*

_____

_____

_____

5. What should be our response to those who serve the church?

*"That you . . . assist her in whatever business she has need of you" (Rom. 16:2). This means
no hierarchy in the church, but we all help one another. "No longer do I call you servants . . .
but I have called you friends" (John 15:15).*

_____

_____

_____

6. How broad was the ministry of Phoebe? How broad should your ministry reach?
How does a person use her spiritual gift of serving?

"She has been a helper of many" (Rom. 16:2).

_____

_____

_____

7. Phoebe was a servant (helper) to Paul, but what was Paul's response?

"For though I am free from all men, I have made myself a servant to all" (1 Cor. 9:19).

_____

_____

_____

8. As we serve other people, we also serve the Lord. How have you served others?
When we serve others in the church, whom are we really serving?

*"If I then, your Lord and Teacher, have washed your feet, you also ought to wash one another's
feet. For I have given you an example, that you should do as I have done to you" (John
13:14–15). "Inasmuch as you did it to one of the least of these My brethren, you did it to Me"
(Matt. 25:40).*

_____

_____

_____

YOUR TIME TO PRAY

Add the following requests to your daily prayer list. As you pray about developing the gift of helps, you will find several things happening in your life: (1) Prayer gives you a desire to use your gift; (2) prayer gives you wisdom to use your gift (James 1:5); (3) prayer influences the lives of those you touch in ministry; (4) God answers by growing your gift; and (5) you grow to maturity in Christ and become more effective in use of all gifts.

1. Ask God to help you see practical things you could do for your family members. *Lord, increase my vision of ways to help those I love.*

2. Yield to God your attitude and prejudices about helping others. *Lord, I'm selfish and I have difficulty helping others; give me a heart to serve others.*

3. Ask God to give you creative ideas to help others in the family. *Lord, show me the best way to help my family so they appreciate what I'm doing and they know I love them.*

4. Pray about the many jobs that need to be done in your church. *Lord, there are so many jobs to do at my church. Show me which ones You want me to do.*

5. Ask God to give you a greater desire to serve in your church and to help you grow your abilities to serve Him. *Lord, You need to give me wisdom to do what You want done and give me grace to do it.*

6. Pray that you grow in character and in all spiritual ministries as you develop your gift of serving. *Lord, I want to be like you; give me a heart to serve others.*

7. Your personal prayer list:

_____

_____

_____

_____

_____

_____

_____

_____

_____

_____

_____

_____

_____

JOURNALING AND MEDITATION

As you study this workbook, think about the things you are learning by writing them down. You will clarify your thoughts as you express them in words. Journaling turns feelings into acts and helps you understand what's happening internally. Actually, your journal—like a diary—is like a mirror that helps you look into your soul.

1. Make a list of all the enjoyable tasks that you look forward to doing each day, each week.

2. Think through the pleasurable tasks at home or church that you like to do. What about the task do you enjoy doing? Write down some of the pleasant experiences you remember. How did they make you feel? What did you learn from doing them? How would you do them differently in the future?

3. Make a list of the unpleasant tasks that you must do each day. How do you feel when you must do something you feel is unpleasant? Write down your experiences. Now determine how you could re-arrange the tasks to make the task more enjoyable. What could you do to change your attitude toward doing unpleasant tasks? Ask God to help you make the work fun.

4. Think through the process of changing your point of view about helping others. How have you changed your mind in the past? How can you change your attitude toward helping and serving people? Write down your thoughts.

5. What journaling can look like:

Day One

Today my daughter called to ask for my ideas for decorating her new home. I love to be needed . . . and wanted. I love to help her decorate and she looks to me for the help she needs. We both win!

Day Two

This journal is a great reminder of how God uses me. I often forget in my "busyness" that serving others is fulfilling and satisfying. A calendar of "helping" shows me where I spend time exercising my gift or if I'm wasting time where I'm really not needed or wanted.

"Lord, please make me a *useful* tool in Your hand."

6. Now, your turn to journal:

_____

_____

_____

_____

LOIS AND EUNICE TAUGHT A YOUNG DISCIPLE

THE SPIRITUAL GIFT OF
TEACHING/MENTORING

Everyone said that Theresa was a natural-born teacher. She approached everything in life analytically; she broke down problems into small steps, then she proceeded to explain to anyone around what she learned. When her children were small, Theresa always taught them new words, constantly pushing to increase their vocabulary. Quickly their words became phrases, and when her children could speak sentences, she began a routine to memorize Bible verses. Theresa's children could count, add, subtract, and multiply quicker than any other children in the neighborhood. It's not that they were naturally smarter, it's just that Theresa pushed them to learn quicker than anyone else.

When the family went on a vacation, Theresa loved to visit museums, historical sites, anything that would increase her knowledge of the world. When the kids were smaller, they dutifully followed her into places they thought were boring and listened to her explain the world around them. Because she married young, and had children early, she never went to college. But when Theresa's children got out of college, she finally saw a way to get the college education she never had.

Even though she started later in life, her insatiable thirst for knowledge helped her get through college in three years, and when she got a teaching job in a local school, she found they required her to keep her certification by working on a master's degree. She got it in two years. Because of Theresa's academic excellence, she was offered a fellowship to work on her doctorate in education. After talking it over with her husband, she accepted the challenge and began working on her degree immediately. Within a short period of time, Theresa finished her dissertation, graduating at the head of her class.

Today, Theresa is an assistant professor of education with a specialty in elementary education. But once she got her doctorate, her desire for knowledge kept pushing her to learn more and more. She became interested in mastering the Bible after she took over a class of young single women. The same passion that drove her to get the doctorate motivated her to learn the Word of God. Within a short period of time, the young single girls were telling others about Theresa's teaching ability, and she was invited to give lectures at a local Bible college in the psychology of learning. That's where she began integrating the Word of God with what she learned at the university. Theresa has found a niche where she can continue to grow as a Bible scholar at the Bible college, while continuing to teach students at the university.

WHAT IS THE GIFT OF TEACHING?

Women with the gift of teaching (1) love to study and clarify truth, (2) feel teaching is foundational to all other gifts, (3) present truth systematically, (4) have a passion to present truth accurately, (5) are intolerant of those who misinterpret truth or communicate truth wrongly, and (6) enjoy listening to others who correctly communicate truth.

UNDERSTANDING THE GIFT OF TEACHING

Every mother has the gift of teaching, for a gracious God knowing the difficulties of life would not give a mother the responsibility of raising a child without giving her the added giftedness to teach that child. But not just mothers have the gift of teaching; every woman has some ability to be a teacher, and that is an important gift. Remember, Paul said, "God has appointed these in the church: first apostles, second prophets, third teachers . . ." (1 Cor. 12:28).

Those who say that teachers are made, not born, are only half right, because all teachers were born, but not necessarily born teachers. The truth is, teachers are both born and made. Anyone can learn to be a better teacher. Our spiritual giftedness of teaching contains both inherited and acquired factors. There are certain temperaments and raw intelligence that teachers have at birth. But they become better teachers by sharpening their skills of communication through hard study, adopting the right role models, and constant practice.

WHO HAS THE SPIRITUAL GIFT OF TEACHING?

Those who love to study and clarify truth. If you have the gift of teaching, you naturally want to study the Bible just to find out new things. You probably like to read, figure out things, and you enjoy learning.

Those who feel teaching is foundational to all the other spiritual gifts. Sometimes the teacher feels that preaching to motivate and exhort is good, but teachers feel that learning is foundational to Christianity, because true faith in Christ is built on knowing the Word of God. When a teacher tries to lead someone to Christ, she makes sure that the convert understands the plan of salvation and understands what he is praying when he receives Christ. In contrast, the person with the spiritual gift of evangelism is more concerned about the experience of receiving Christ, rather than what the person knows and what he understands.

Those who tend to present truth systematically. Teachers write out lesson plans, making sure that one point logically leads to another; they end their lessons with conclusions. Even when illustrations are used, they tell stories to illustrate truth, rather than telling stories simply to move emotions or produce feelings as an evangelist or exhorter might do.

Therefore, those with the spiritual gift of teaching are concerned that people learn. Their primary thrust in the classroom is that pupils acquire the lessons being presented.

Those with a passion to communicate truth accurately. Teachers usually correct errors they perceive in others, and they go to great lengths to make sure their pupils know the facts accurately and that they do not "misunderstand" the lesson that is being presented.

Those who are intolerant of others who misinterpret truth or communicate truth wrongly. Teachers are concerned when they hear someone misinterpret a verse, or take a verse out of context. They get upset when people hold to the wrong interpretation, or when a teacher leaves the wrong impression.

Those who enjoy listening to others communicate correct knowledge of the truth. Just as "birds of a feather flock together," teachers enjoy listening to other good teachers who have their same passion and value to communicate truth.

WATCHING FOR THE GIFT OF TEACHING IN YOUNG GIRLS

1. They explain things to their friends, brothers and sisters, even adults.

2. They have a natural desire to read and they are self-motivated to prepare their lessons in school.

3. They like to write their thoughts down, i.e., diaries, journals, notes, letters, etc.

4. They ask a lot of questions of parents and older adults, wanting to know reasons for things.

5. They like quiz games in which they have to remember information.

6. They have a keen motivation to understand the reasons behind things, so they naturally like to read, study, explore, or examine.

7. On vacations, they look into the background of places, events, or people.

HOW IMPORTANT IS THE SPIRITUAL GIFT OF TEACHING?

Those with the gift of teaching are extremely important in God's order of ministry, because teaching is listed high in the order of gifts. "God has appointed these in the church: first apostles, second prophets, third teachers . . ." (1 Cor. 12:28). Because the work of the kingdom is based upon truth, and a church can never be founded upon error, the gift of teachers is imperative for each church.

Who has the spiritual gift of teaching? As previously stated, every mother has the gift of teaching, for a gracious God would not give a woman the responsibility of a child without giving her the added giftedness to teach that child. But not only mothers have the gift of teaching; every woman has some ability to be a teacher because all are commanded to teach: "Teaching them to observe all things that I have commanded you" (Matt. 28:20).

Since God doesn't give you a task without His enablement, then all believers have the ability to teach.

Can you grow in your ability to teach? Your giftedness, which comes from God, can grow in its usefulness. "Earnestly desire the best gifts" (1 Cor. 12:31). Obviously, many grandmothers are very gifted in handling children, much more so than the young mother who has just starting learning how to handle her first baby. The grandmother has grown in her spiritual giftedness of teaching children.

LOIS AND EUNICE WERE TEACHERS

"Then he [Paul] came to Derbe and Lystra. And behold, a certain disciple was there, named Timothy, the son of a certain Jewish woman who believed but his father was Greek. He was well spoken of by the brethren who were at Lystra and Iconium. Paul wanted to have him go on with him. And he took him and circumcised him because of the Jews who were in that region, for they all knew that his father was a Greek" (Acts 16:1–3).

"When I call to remembrance the genuine faith that is in you, which dwelt first in your grandmother Lois and your mother Eunice, and I am persuaded is in you also" (2 Tim. 1:5).

"But you must continue in the things which you have learned and been assured of, knowing from whom you have learned them, and that from childhood you have known the Holy Scriptures, which are able to make you wise for salvation through faith which is in Christ Jesus" (2 Tim. 3:14–15).

To study teaching giftedness in women, look at two women with very little culture, very little religious support, and the prospects of being marooned in an isolated mountain village in Asia Minor for life. Lois, the grandmother, and Eunice, her daughter, were sincere Jewish followers of Jehovah, but both women married Gentile husbands. There was no mention of a synagogue in their town of Lystra, suggesting the number of Jewish families was small (twelve Jewish families are required to organize a synagogue). With little hope in life, other than to influence society through a child, Lois and Eunice poured their best into young Timothy, and through their giftedness of teaching, these women influenced the world.

How do we know they were teachers? Lois and Eunice were not called teachers, so how can we say they had the gift of teaching? Teaching is not just measured by how well you instruct, but is measured by how well your pupil learns. Timothy, the son of Eunice and grandson of Lois, was an outstanding student. Paul describes him, "Continue in the things which you have learned and been assured of, knowing from whom you have learned them, and that from childhood you have known the Holy Scriptures, which are able to make you wise for salvation through faith which is in Christ Jesus" (2 Tim. 3:14–15). The women made sure that Timothy knew the Scriptures because they taught him the Word of God from his infancy.

What was their curriculum? Mothers teach many of the basic functions of life to their children; in fact, mothers are responsible for more that the child learns than any other human in life. Lois and Eunice taught young Timothy many things, but their most outstanding lessons come from the Scriptures, "from childhood you have known the Holy Scriptures" (2 Tim. 3:15).

What you teach your children determines what is important to your life. The child will learn about horses if the mother constantly talks about riding and caring for horses and she always points out pictures of horses in the magazines. Any passion of the mother influences her children. The light in the eye of the mother shines deeply into the heart of the child. The light of God's Word in the hearts of Lois and Eunice penetrated Timothy's soul.

How well did they teach the Scriptures? They taught the Old Testament to Timothy. However, the women did more than just teach some information about the Old Testament, they taught him what was in each book of the Old Testament. Paul used the word *gramma* (scripture), which is plural, suggesting Lois and Eunice taught all the books of the Old Testament.

Timothy probably did more than memorize the books in order, something our children learn in Sunday school. He also probably did more than memorize the general content of each book; also something our children learn in Sunday school. Because most young Hebrew children memorized the entire book of Leviticus—word for word—Timothy probably could recite this book by memory. Reading the letters that Paul wrote to Timothy, you get the impression that Timothy had memorized much of the Old Testament and knew its content well.

WEAKNESSES OR DANGERS OF THE GIFT OF TEACHING

Some common weaknesses associated with the spiritual gift of teaching are: (1) greater interest in interpretation of Scripture than application, (2) pride over knowledge, (3) concentration on factual details, rather than giving attention to the issues of life, and (4) greater concern for truth than for individuals.

How did the Scriptures make a deep impression on Timothy? Lois and Eunice had taught the Bible so well to young Timothy that a biblical worldview influenced his outlook on life. There are some children that only learn Bible stories and verses, when, in fact, the Bible does not influence their life. Not so with Timothy. When Paul said, "From childhood you have known the Holy Scriptures" (2 Tim. 3:15), the word *known* is *oida,* which means innate knowledge. Timothy had a grasp of the Bible content, but in the process the Bible captured Timothy's life. He had a biblical understanding of life and interpreted life by biblical principles.

Which woman was the teacher? Both Lois and Eunice were teachers. One might think that just Eunice the mother was the teacher of her son Timothy, but this is most likely not the case. When Paul said "knowing from whom [plural] you have learned them" (2 Tim. 3:14), he implied both Lois and Eunice were his teachers. When one woman left off teaching, the other took up the instructive path. Young Timmy didn't have a chance with two women hovering about to teach him the Word of God.

What was the greatest result of their teaching? The greatest result was Timothy's salvation. Probably Lois and Eunice had many great qualities, as all women have more than one great characteristic. Perhaps one was an immaculate housekeeper, while the other was a great cook. Perhaps one always dressed fashionably, while the other was an excellent manager of the household. Whatever their great qualities, there is one thing they had in common: They were both excellent teachers and it was evident in the changed life of their pupil Timothy. They taught "the Holy Scriptures, which are able to make you wise for salvation" (2 Tim. 3:15).

After your children are raised and you sit in retirement with your husband, how would you like for your life to be remembered? Will you remember your first home after you were married? Will you remember the coordinated outfits you wore to church? How many of the wonderful meals that you have prepared will be remembered? Obviously, the greatest legacy you can leave in life is your children who know and live the Word of God. Like it or not, your contribution to life will be measured by the contribution of your children after you're gone.

We give so little time teaching those into whose hands we will commit all.
Socrates

WHAT RESOURCES DID THESE TEACHERS HAVE?

When Lois and Eunice began their task to make sure that young Timothy became a godly man, God sent them many helpers to influence young Timothy.

First, they had each other. The faith of both these women "rubbed off" on the young Timothy: "The genuine faith that is in you, which dwelt first in your grandmother Lois and your mother Eunice" (2 Tim. 1:5). When you want to influence your children for godliness, remember godly influence is like the measles. You can't give it unless you have it. In the same way, you influence the lives of your children by the way you live, not just by theoretical lessons.

Second, they had the Bible. Even though Lois and Eunice were the human instruments to bring Timothy to salvation, what they taught—the Word of God—was responsible for his salvation. Paul reminds Timothy, "You have known the Holy Scriptures, which are able to make you wise for salvation through faith which is in Christ Jesus" (2 Tim. 3:15).

Paul helped them. Even though Paul arrived on the scene when Timothy was approximately sixteen years old, he notes his influence on the salvation of young Timothy. "Paul . . . To Timothy, a true son in the faith" (1 Tim. 1:1–2). Whereas Paul may have been the one actually to lead Timothy to receive Christ, many others had laid the foundation for that experience. Technically, during this time of transition from Old Testament law to New Testament grace, Timothy probably enjoyed salvation as a Jew—as did his mother and grandmother—because they had honestly believed in God through the Old Testament Scriptures. But when Paul preached Jesus Christ to them, they believed in Jesus the Messiah and were converted.

What obstacles did they overcome to teach Timothy? Just because Lois and Eunice had the gift of teaching doesn't mean it was easy to be a teacher. Both times in the Bible when the father is mentioned, it is noted that he was not a believer; "His [Timothy's] father was Greek" (Acts 16:1). "Paul...took him [Timothy] and circumcised him [Timothy] . . . for they all knew that his father was Greek" (Acts 16:3). Just as we hear the phrase, "like father, like son," it also is true, "like mother, like daughter." Lois had originally married an unsaved Greek, but her faith was so strong she overcame the non-Jewish influence in her home to continue living for God. In a town where there were few Jewish young men for a young Jewish girl to marry—or Lois's husband insisted otherwise—the young daughter, Eunice, also followed the example of her mother and married a Greek.

Because Timothy's father is never mentioned by name in the Bible, most think the father had little influence on Timothy, at least not the influence that his mother, Eunice had. While the father wasn't a positive influence on Timothy, he also wasn't an obstacle to his faith. Notice how Timothy's father influenced his training.

The father allowed Lois and Eunice to teach their biblical faith to Timothy. A Greek father could have insisted that young Timothy be educated according to the Roman tradition of Caesar worship, but apparently he didn't. Timothy is described as "the son of a certain Jewish woman who believed" (Acts 16:1).

The father didn't prohibit his wife's belief. Timothy's father first allowed his wife to practice her Jewish tradition, then, second, allowed his son to be taught the Jewish tradition. Eunice is first introduced in Scripture as "a Jewess and a believer" (Acts 16:1 NIV).

The father allowed Bible teaching. In a Roman home, very few women could read and write, therefore Roman mothers were not the teachers of the children. Wealthy homes hired a teacher who was brought into the home to teach the young boys. Sometimes a slave who could read and write taught the children. On other occasions, young boys were sent to a private school for tutoring. But Timothy's father allowed his wife and mother-in-law to teach his son the Word of God. Timothy's father must have understood the strength that would come to his son by education in general and learning the Word of God in particular, so he allowed Bible teaching.

The father allowed religious attendance. There probably wasn't a synagogue in Lystra, but there was a Jewish community that would have gathered for prayers and Bible reading. This religious community knew Timothy, because he had attended their religious gatherings, "He was well spoken of by the brethren who were at Lystra" (Acts 16:2). The father allowed Timothy to attend the Jewish gatherings.

WHAT IS TEACHING?

Teaching is not what you do in front of a class, even though many people think a woman's teaching ability is measured by how well she performs in front of the class. Therefore, the success of teaching is not measured by what you do in the classroom, it is measured by what happens in the lives and thinking of your pupils.

> TEACHING IS THE PREPARATION AND GUIDANCE OF LEARNING ACTIVITIES.

There are three steps to understanding teaching. Each step is like a leg of a three-legged stool: Without any one of the legs, the stool will collapse. Each depends upon the others to accomplish its task.

Preparation. The first step of teaching is preparation. Recently I (Elmer) was on my way to an early Sunday morning prayer meeting at our church. A Sunday school teacher of five-year-olds stopped me to invite me to drop by her class after prayer meeting for some milk and Oreo cookies. Who could resist such a temptation?

I arrived at the classroom and was talking with the two ladies who taught the class when a five-year-old girl arrived at the door. One of the ladies excused herself saying, "I must go because teaching begins the moment the first pupil arrives in my class." I disagreed with what she said, but, being appreciative of the Oreos and milk, I didn't say anything. I only smiled. But the other lady spoke up.

"I disagree . . . teaching doesn't begin when the first pupil arrives," she emphatically declared after her partner left. "Teaching begins when I arrive in the classroom to prepare the class."

Again, I disagreed but only smiled to myself, not wanting to be negative to what she said. I personally believe teaching begins much earlier. As a matter of fact, when a teacher first opens her Bible or teacher's manual during the week to begin preparing her lesson, that is when teaching begins. The way you prepare determines the way you teach. And what you prepare determines what you teach. The applications you prepare determine the applications you teach. Everything you do in preparation influences the outcome of your teaching. And those who do not prepare are not very effective in their teaching. What else can we say about Bible preparation?

> BECAUSE THE WAY YOU STUDY DETERMINES THE WAY YOU TEACH, THERE ARE NO NATURALLY GREAT BIBLE TEACHERS; THERE ARE ONLY BIBLE STUDENTS.

Guidance. The second aspect of teaching is really the process of guiding pupils. No teacher can make a pupil learn, just as no one can make a horse drink water. But you can help the process by putting salt on the horse's tongue; then the horse will do its own drinking. So the teacher can only guide pupils; they will do their own learning. Therefore, *teaching is guidance, or leading pupils.*

Philip was a layman who would shortly become an evangelist in the church. The Spirit of God led him to a desert road where he saw the Ethiopian eunuch—the treasurer of Ethiopia—reading from the Old Testament. Philip ran to ask the Ethiopian, "Do you understand what you are reading?" (Acts 8:30). Philip was doing what all teachers should do. We should ask our pupils questions to get them to think about the Word of God. The Ethiopian was reading the Word of God but did not understand what he was reading. He answered Philip's question, "How can I, unless someone guides me" (Acts 8:31).

The Ethiopian was asking for a teacher to guide him. The secret to teaching is not what you tell your pupils, but how you guide your pupils to learn. When Philip guided the Ethiopian into the Word of God, he also guided him to salvation. As a result of Philip's teaching, the Ethiopian was converted and baptized.

Those who fish in the north woods will employ a guide to take them to the proper lake to fish. It is assumed that the guide *knows the way*, the guide *knows where fish are*, and the guide *knows how to catch fish*. What a fishing guide does for the fisherman is what the teacher does for students. The guide gets you there, but you must catch the fish. The teacher may present a lesson, but pupils do their own learning.

Learning activities. If all we teach is knowledge, all our pupils learn are facts. If all we teach them are habits, all they learn are skills. But teaching is more than talking about facts, and learning is more than acquiring skills. Our students must interact with facts, gain skills, gain wisdom, and become active in the learning process. They must experience the Bible to learn the Bible.

PRACTICAL TAKE-AWAYS

The following questions were written for group discussion with a Sunday school class or Bible study. These questions are written in the first person to help you personalize your answers and apply them to your life.

1. *Can I be an effective teacher without the spiritual giftedness of teaching*? Many women have been great teachers in Sunday school or Bible classes, yet their dominant spiritual gift was not teaching. Rather, their giftedness was probably exhortation, which means they communicate the lesson with positive motivation, wanting the student to live the lesson out in life. (The gift of exhortation produces a woman who is both positive and practical in emphasis.) Usually the teacher with the gift of exhortation does not have a great passion to study, but she has a great passion for changing the lives of her pupils. Even though the church calls her "teacher" or Sunday school teacher, she influences pupils through her spiritual gift of exhortation. God uses exhorters as well as teachers in the lives of their students because they help their pupils live in a positive and practical way.

HOW IS THE GIFT OF TEACHING EXPRESSED?

The woman with the gift of teaching: instructs in Bible, handwork, worship, games, or group activities. She teaches piano, computer skills, driving, sports, or knitting. She is a superintendent, teacher, helper, counselor, or mentor. She teaches one person, a small class, or a large group. She teaches by television, by telephone, or by the Internet. She teaches babies, children, teens, adults, or senior citizens.

2. *What other gifts can I have, yet be an effective teacher*? God has given the church many teachers, but each one teaches in a different way and each one has different results. The teacher who has a dominant gift of mercy-showing will spend a lot of time counseling students, and the teacher with the dominant gift of helps will do a lot of things for her students. Because everyone's background is different and everyone's home environment is not the same, everyone will express her gift of teaching differently. Because everyone's education and temperament are different, everyone will teach with different tempos and passion. Paul noted, "There are different ways spiritual gifts operate, but it is the same God who works through that gift" (1 Cor. 12:6, author's paraphrase).

THREE-STEP BIBLE STUDY

Step One, read the questions to get you thinking about God's name.

Step Two, analyze the verses with each question to see what the Bible says about the question.

Step Three, write your answers in the space provided.

1. **Lois and Eunice are not called teachers, so how do we know they had the gift of teaching? Teaching is not just measured by how well you instruct, it is measured by how well pupils learn.**

    "But you must continue in the things which you have learned and been assured of, knowing from whom you have learned them, and that from childhood you have known the Holy Scriptures, which are able to make you wise for salvation through faith which is in Christ Jesus" (2 Tim 3:14–15). "When I call to remembrance the genuine faith that is in you, which dwelt first in your grandmother Lois and your mother Eunice, and I am persuaded is in you also. Therefore I remind you to stir up the gift of God which is in you" (2 Tim. 1:5–6).

    _____

    _____

    _____

2. **What was the content of their teaching?**

    "From childhood you have known the Holy Scriptures" (2 Tim. 3:15).

    _____

    _____

    _____

3. **How much of the Bible did they teach?**

    "Scriptures" (2 Tim. 3:15). Gramma is plural, meaning they taught all the books of the Old Testament.

    _____

    _____

    _____

4. **How well did they teach? Timothy did more than memorize the Scriptures. He *knew* (innate knowledge), which meant the Bible had become second nature to him.**

    "But you must continue in the things which you have learned and been assured of, knowing from whom you have learned them" (2 Tim. 3:14).

    _____

    _____

    _____

5. **What was the result of their teaching?**

    "The Holy Scriptures, which are able to make you wise for salvation" (2 Tim. 3:15).

    _____

    _____

    _____

6. **Who or what was responsible for the conversion of Timothy?**

"The genuine faith that is in you, which dwelt first in your grandmother Lois and your mother Eunice" (2 Tim. 1:5).

"The Holy Scriptures, which are able to make you wise for salvation though faith which is in Christ Jesus" (2 Tim. 3:15).

"Paul . . . To Timothy, a true son in the faith" (1 Tim. 1:1–2).

_____

_____

_____

7. **How important is teaching in God's order?**

"God has appointed these in the church: first apostles, second prophets, third teachers . . ." (1 Cor. 12:28).

_____

_____

_____

8. **How can we grow in our ability to teach?**

"Earnestly desire the best gifts" (1 Cor. 12:31).

_____

_____

_____

YOUR TIME TO PRAY

Add the following requests to your daily prayer list. As you pray about developing the gift of teaching, you will find several things happening in your life: (1) Prayer gives you a desire to use your gift; (2) prayer gives you wisdom to use your gift (James 1:5); (3) prayer influences the lives of those you touch in ministry; (4) God answers by growing your gift; and (5) you grow to maturity in Christ and become more effective in use of all gifts.

1. Ask God to give you a greater curiosity about things, so that you spend more time looking up the background of events, places, and people. *Lord, give me a holy curiosity about important things I need to know, and help me trust You about things I don't need to know, then give me wisdom to distinguish between the two.*

2. Ask God to increase your desire to study and master the Word of God, because you will have a greater desire to teach if you have a growing desire to learn the Bible. *Lord, give me a holy hunger for the Scriptures, then help me find time to study Your Word.*

3. Pray for discernment to understand the reasons for the events that surround your life so that you can understand what is happening and can explain them to others. *Lord, open my eyes to see what is happening around me. Help me to understand and trust You more.*

4. Ask God to help you see the needs in your family and in others, then ask Him to help you apply the Scriptures to their lives. When you realize how the Bible can help them, you will want to teach them. *Lord, may I see the needs of others through Your eyes.*

5. Pray for a burden to share the Word of God with your family and others. You will become a teacher when you feel an obligation to share the Word of God with others. *Lord, I will be a teacher if that is Your will; give me a burden to do what You want.*

6. Your personal prayer list:

_____

_____

_____

JOURNALING AND MEDITATION

As you study this workbook, think about the things you are learning by writing them down. You will clarify your thoughts as you express them in words. Journaling turns feelings into acts and helps you understand what's happening internally. Actually, your journal—like a diary—is like a mirror that helps you look into your soul.

1. Make a list in your journal of the things you need to study, or you would like to study. Now put them in order of priority and write a compelling reason for studying the first topic.

2. Think of the teacher who made the greatest influence on your life. Write out the reasons and/or ways that teacher influenced you. List the ways you could be like that teacher. Now pray and ask God to help you influence others, the way that teacher influenced you.

3. Write down one incident in which God has used you when you shared something with a child. How did you feel? Would you like to do that on a regular basis? How could you do it?

4. Write down one incident when you were used of God to teach a group or to share something with more than one person. How did you do it? How did you feel? How could you do it again?

5. Some people don't want to teach because they had an unpleasant experience(s) in school. Think through any school experiences that may have turned you off to teaching. How could you reverse your feelings about teaching? How could you become a more effective teacher?

6. What journaling could look like:

Day One

Buck Hatch loved to teach. There was never a doubt that he was a "gifted" teacher and seemed to have a hunger to see students grasp the lessons, making them their own. We have forgotten most of the class material and notes taken, but one lesson stays with me to this day.

The class was absorbed in talking among ourselves, even during his lecture, and we were not paying attention. He stopped teaching for a few moments until we settled down, but soon we went back to our conversations among ourselves. Quietly, and almost tearfully, Mr. Hatch closed his notebook and put his books and papers in his briefcase. He bowed his head. When he lifted his eyes to us again, he was barely heard to say, "I'm sorry. I've failed you as your teacher today. Your lack of attention is my fault. Class dismissed." We were stunned. He left the classroom and we just sat in ashamed silence.

We learned that there are many ways to get a point across, and a gifted teacher communicates many lessons besides the assigned curriculum. (Ruth Towns)

Day Two

I was looking through all the Mother's Day cards when it really hit me. My mother died a year ago! There was no one to send the card to. I stood motionless, almost holding my breath. I missed my mother. She taught me so much that I've tried to pass on to my children . . .

- . . . always push your grocery cart on the right-hand side of the aisle as though you are driving a car.
- . . . when on a date, don't order messy food like spaghetti or chili dogs. You'll be embarrassed.
- . . . if your curfew is 11:00, you would be wise to come inside at 10:35.
- . . . work hard—do your *best*.
- . . . God has a special person for you to marry.
- . . . guard your reputation. Your name has integrity and people expect you to walk "uprightly."
- . . . people have memories—don't say something you don't want remembered.
- . . . what goes around, comes around.

By her example I learned:
. . . take time to be holy.
. . . "beauty is as beauty does."
. . . if you can't take Jesus with you, don't go!
. . . smell good.
. . . find the Lord first in the morning and praise Him.
. . . smile — people like to be around happy people.
. . . appreciate little things — the smell of a rose, a baby's out-stretched arms, fresh, crisp fall air, a rainbow. (Ruth Towns)

7. Now, your turn to journal:

_____

_____

_____

_____

_____

_____

_____

_____

_____

_____

_____

_____

_____

_____

_____

_____

_____

_____

_____

_____

_____

_____

_____

_____

ESTHER HAD A POSITIVE PLAN THAT WORKED

THE SPIRITUAL GIFT OF
EXHORTATION

Joyce has the gift of exhortation, which means she has always been positive and practical. She goes about her work with a perennial smile and she speaks to everyone. Her infectious smile makes most people smile back. Recently, Joyce encountered a crisis in her family. She discovered her fifth-grade boy had gone home with a friend, and each of them drank a bottle of beer. Joyce's husband was angry, because as a child he had grown up in a home where his father was an alcoholic. Joyce's husband was saved—literally saved from alcoholism—when he was converted to Christ and he reacted negatively to liquor. He hates the "stuff" and almost hates anyone who drinks. When he found out his son had drunk a beer, he wanted to beat him with a belt, just like his father had punished him. While her husband became violent and emotional, Joyce approached it with a cool head. Her husband's emotional reaction would have ended in severe punishment for their son, if it had not been for Joyce. Joyce felt her husband's harsh approach would not solve the problem, and might even drive their son into lifelong rebellion with an addictive habit. Her husband has a spiritual gift of prophecy, which has a low tolerance for anyone who violates God's standard of righteousness. When he found out, his first reaction was to "spank him so hard" he'd never want another bottle of beer. Then, the father wanted to ground his son for a year so he couldn't get to the stuff and he'd remember to never do it again. And of course, the father didn't want his son ever again to play with the boy who gave him beer, or ever to go to that home again.

"He's already done it," Joyce argued with her husband. "He's young, impressionable, and wants to be one of the gang."

Joyce entertained thoughts that alcoholism might be in the family bloodline and that her son might become an alcoholic because his grandfather was one. But she quickly dismissed those thoughts, thinking anyone could be taught to live on a higher level above alcohol, if only the right teacher would help mold their outlook. Joyce determined to be that positive influence on her son.

Joyce's positive nature controlled her outlook throughout the crisis. She realized her son was a good boy who drank because of bad influences. She also realized her son had never been taught the evils of alcohol and its effect on his father's family. Because she's practical, she devised a plan to communicate to their son why they both totally reject drinking alcohol and make sure he wouldn't do it again.

"When we see on television pictures of violence or drunkenness associated with beer," Joyce told her husband, "we'll remind him about the consequences of drinking alcohol." The father expressed his spiritual gift by sitting down with his son to warn him about the grandfather's alcoholism that destroyed his life and his home. Joyce studied ahead in the family Bible readings to find an alcohol-related passage. She planned questions for family discussion to give her son reasons he shouldn't drink. After studying the Bible, both Joyce and her husband prayed aloud in front of him that he would be alcohol-free. They wanted their son to feel their passionate rejection of alcohol.

Because Joyce and her husband have different spiritual giftedness, they react to problems differently and they attempt to solve problems differently. If you have the gift of exhortation, you ought to know how you look at life positively, and you ought to understand that other people don't react to life the way you do.

UNDERSTANDING THE GIFT OF EXHORTATION

The woman with the spiritual gift of exhortation is both positive and practical in interpreting life. She stimulates faith and always sees the glass half full, not half empty. She gets excited about helping others live by biblical principles.

"We have been given different spiritual gifts according to the grace of God . . . if you have the gift of exhortation, then use the gift of exhortation"
(Rom. 12:6, 8, author's translation).

What does the Bible mean by exhortation? Since exhortation means different things to different individuals, we ought to study how the Bible uses the term. The term *exhortation* comes from the Greek *parakaieo* which means "to call aside, appeal to, to help, to instruct." A dictionary definition is "conveying urgent advice or recommendation." The NIV translates it as "encouragement." "We have different gifts, according to the grace given us . . . if it is encouraging, let him encourage" (Rom. 12:6, 8 NIV).

WHAT IS THE GIFT OF EXHORTATION?

The woman with the gift of exhortation (1) will usually encourage others, (2) is excited about practical principles that work in life, (3) uses positive (rather than negative) motivation on others, (4) interprets life by biblical principles that apply to Christian living, (5) sees the practical side of Christianity when she studies Scriptures, and (6) has great faith in the ability of God to work in the lives of her children and others.

To understand an exhorter, look at what she has done. She is probably not a woman who will go door-to-door getting petitions signed about an ungodly problem in the neighborhood. A woman with the gift of prophecy will do that. The exhorter will come up with a positive way to attack the problem. Neither does the exhorter run to the church kitchen to wipe a counter or help in serving the meal at the church supper as a woman with the gift of helps might do. However, when an exhorter sees a long line of people at the coffeepot being served one at a time, she finds a practical way to move the line along more quickly. She will place the cream and sugar on another table to move the line along, then will pour the coffee into cups and hand them out so the line can move even more quickly. The exhorter will not volunteer for Tuesday night evangelistic visitation because she does not have a dominant gift of evangelism, but she might develop a plan for a few women to mail invitations into the neighborhood, inviting them to church.

HOW THE GIFT OF EXHORTATION WORKS

She teaches Sunday school, Bible studies, and VBS. She uses positive motivation on her family. She mentors, coaches sport teams, works with AWANA or Girl Scouts, and helps her children's teachers. She sends cards, advises young brides, and helps people solve problems. She's a secretary, administrative assistant, or team cheerleader. She's a neighbor who will always help.

ESTHER WAS AN EXHORTER

Esther was a young Jewish girl raised in Shushan, the capital of Persia. She was only one of millions of Jews driven from their homeland. The Bible tells us nothing about her parents, but says that she was raised by Mordecai, her cousin. Because Mordecai was a government official and wise counselor, when the king announced a beauty pageant to select the next queen, Mordecai told Esther to enter, but wisely told her to keep her nationality hidden. Because of her beauty and charm, Esther became the next queen. If you close your eyes, you can see her: tall, slim, stately, and she naturally fills out an elegant dress. Esther walks gracefully like a model.

Haman, the prime minister of Persia, hated Jews and deceptively got a law passed that anyone who killed a Jew on a certain date could plunder the Jew's estate and keep any wealth he could find from the dead Jew's home, even keeping the home itself. When the Jews faced a national crisis that could have wiped every trace of Jewish heritage from the earth, Esther used her traits of "exhortation" to solve the problem in a practical way, then developed a solution to save the Jewish nation.

How did Esther get her gift of exhortation? Apparently, she was greatly influenced by her cousin Mordecai. When he is first mentioned in Scripture, he devises a positive way for Esther to become influential, i.e., to become queen. Then cousin Mordecai recommended she not try to overcome her ethnic background, but he approached it practically, suggesting she not mention it. "Esther had not revealed her people or family, for Mordecai had charged her not to reveal it" (Esth. 2:10).

How was Esther's gift of exhortation first revealed? When Mordecai found out that the Jews could be killed, he immediately put on sackcloth (a symbol of repentance) and began praying for an answer, because, "Letters were sent. . . to destroy, to kill, and to annihilate all the Jews, both young and old, little children and women in one day . . . and to plunder their possessions" (Esth. 3:13). Many people when faced with a problem could become angry, curse God, or hate those that threatened them. Mordecai took the problem to God in prayer. While many come to God to solve a problem, those with the gift of exhortation rise from their knees to solve the problem in a positive way, as did Esther. When she saw Mordecai in sackcloth and ashes, she sent him clean clothes to wear, her practical response.

The messenger returned to tell Esther of the severity of imminent disaster. Mordecai warned Esther that she would not be protected, even though hidden in the palace. "Do not think in your heart that you will escape in the king's palace any more than all the other Jews" (Esth. 4:13).

When Esther understood the gravity of the situation, her first response was to pray, just as Mordecai had done. "Go, gather all the Jews . . . and fast for me; neither eat nor drink for three days, night or day. My maids and I will fast likewise" (Esth. 4:16).

Fasting does a couple of things for you when facing a problem. First, fasting may move God to intervene—change the circumstances to solve the problem. Second, when you fast, God gives you great insight on how to solve a problem. It is here that God gave Esther a practical plan to solve the problem. Whether Esther came up with a practical way to solve the problem from her spiritual giftedness, or from fasting, is not the issue. The answer is that after fasting and prayer, Esther knew what to do.

How did Esther attack the problem facing the Jews? The wisdom of Esther is seen in the strategy she developed. She knew that prayer was mandatory and should come first, but praying was not enough. Note the following:

WHAT PRAYER DID NOT DO

1. Prayer did not make the king call her.
2. Prayer did not change the edict.
3. Prayer did not eliminate Haman.
4. Prayer did not make the problem go away.
5. Prayer did not motivate God to do a miracle.

Because of prayer, God gave Esther a strategy to tell the king about the problem and then God turned the king's heart sympathetically to the Jews' crisis. Prayer moved the king to execute Haman. Prayer motivated Esther to come up with a positive plan for how the Jews could save themselves, and prayer motivated the king to implement Esther's plan. Finally, prayer brought glory to God and many became believers in the Lord God of Israel.

WHAT PRAYER DID

1. Prayer gave Esther a strategy to solve the problem.
2. Prayer gave her a receptive audience with her husband.
3. Prayer gave circumstances a desirable solution.
4. Prayer gave her unity with her husband.

Note the practical things Esther did to approach and solve the problem:

Esther wore the right clothes. A woman knows that "man looks at the outward appearance, but the LORD looks at the heart" (1 Sam. 16:7). And while some women become so spiritual that the only thing they see in that verse is God's looking at the heart, Esther understood that a woman can get on the right side of a man by the clothes she wears. What did she do? "Esther put on her royal robes" (Esth. 5:1). Can we not imagine that she fixed her hair the way the king liked, and that she made sure that her face was as attractive as the king liked? She knew to get something from the king, she had to appeal to the king.

Esther stood in the right place. There was a place in the palace where people waited who came to see the king. She didn't try to approach the king by an alternate manner, nor did she try to use any influence with a guard or member of the king's court to get to the king. She stood with those who wanted an audience with the king. She "stood in the inner court of the king's palace, across from the king's house" (Esth. 5:1). We can imagine her beauty, poise, and attractiveness as she stood, calmly waiting for the king to see her, and to extend to her his scepter.

Esther had warned Mordecai that if she went in to see the king, and he rejected her by not extending the scepter, she could be put to death. Whether that would have happened is not the issue. Most women know how to get to a man, and Esther used every positive and practical device at her hand.

Esther understood the positive virtue of enticement. When she appeared before King Ahasuerus (secular name, Xerxes), he immediately extended his scepter when he saw his wife standing there in her beauty. Like any curious husband, he immediately asked, "What do you want?"

Esther was too wise to blurt out her request in panic; Haman, the prime minister—her enemy—was probably standing there, and could refute anything that she said. Also, Esther didn't have the spiritual giftedness of prophecy. She didn't criticize the royal edict, for to criticize his law was to criticize the king. She didn't want to put him in a defensive role.

Esther invited her husband to a lavish feast in her palace that evening. Obviously, the meal was already in preparation as she stood before the king, because food would have been cooking as she invited the king. This reveals faith by Esther that her plan would work. Esther didn't wait for a part of her plan to work before implementing more. By faith she put her whole practical strategy into operation.

Esther killed her enemy with kindness. Haman was the human instrument that Satan was using to destroy all the Jews and the godly line of Messiah. If the Jews were destroyed, Jesus would not have been born. The Bible doesn't say Esther hated Haman, it doesn't describe her reaction. Whatever her feeling, she swallowed it. She invited Haman to the feast that evening with the king.

How many women have hurt their husbands because they haven't liked her husband's boss, and refused to have him into her home for a meal? Or, how many wives have refused to go out to restaurants with their husbands for sales contacts because they didn't like a person, or they selfishly wanted to spend all their time on their affairs. Not so Esther. She invited her enemy to her home for a meal; literally, she would kill him with kindness.

The soft music in the background from the king's musicians set the right mood and the wind blowing through sheer window curtains must have created a romantic evening. The meal must have gone well, and the king must have enjoyed every morsel. Everything was perfect, and when the meal was over the king asked, "So now tell me . . . what do you want?"

But Esther knew that the question with eternal consequences must be answered in the correct way at the correct time, when the king was in the right mood, and when the king was ready to grant her request. Esther didn't answer the king's question the way he phrased it. She didn't tell him what she wanted to say. Esther asked the king to return the next night for another banquet.

> Don't blurt out important requests in haphazard ways. The more important a request, the more preparation you must make to get the correct response.

What happens when practical plans are messed up? The enemy, it seems, always knows how to mess up the "best laid plans of mice and men [ladies too]." The king did not sleep well that night. Some have suggested that Esther was not a good cook and the king couldn't sleep because of indigestion. When he couldn't sleep, he called for some dusty old annals to be read to him. He probably thought these dry court proceedings would put him to sleep. It was there the king discovered a footnote in history, that two of the king's officers had tried to poison him, but Mordecai had discovered the plot and saved his life. The king inquired as to what was done to reward Mordecai for saving his life. He was told that nothing had been done.

A few days earlier when Haman was on his way to the palace, he saw Mordecai at the gate. As the crowd fell on their faces to worship Haman, Mordecai didn't bow. Being true to God's commandments, Mordecai worshiped only the Lord. In fury, Haman ordered the building of a gallows seventy-five feet tall, where he planned to hang Mordecai.

On the morning after Esther's feast—Haman had enjoyed the feast with the king—Haman arrived early into the presence of the king. King Ahasuerus asked, "What should be done for the man the king wishes to honor?"

Haman was sure the king wanted to honor him, so he spared no details. "Dress this man in clothes you have worn," Haman suggested. "Put him on your royal white horse, and have a servant walk before him shouting to the city that this is the man the king wants to honor." This is equivalent to dressing a man in Michael Jordan's uniform he wore when he won his last NBA championship and driving that man in the president's limousine in a ticker tape parade down the streets of New York. The king smiled, because he liked Haman's suggestion.

"You!" the king appointed Haman. "You go and honor Mordecai the way you suggested."

God's humor is revealed in the sovereign way He twists events against the evil intention of His enemies. Haman was utterly embarrassed all day long as he honored his enemy Mordecai by leading him through the city on the king's horse. One wonders if he led the horse past the gallows that were being built to hang Mordecai. Probably not!

When Haman got home that evening, he complained to his wife of his humiliation. But she was not a mercy shower, neither was she an exhorter. Haman's wife had the gift of prophecy. She said, "You should have listened to me . . ." the favorite phrase of the wife with the gift of prophecy who usually fusses at her husband. "Didn't I tell you that Mordecai would be the death of you yet?" Little did she know that in her anger she had predicted what would happen later that evening. And almost immediately, the king's servants arrived at Haman's house to take him to the feast at Esther's palace.

Esther had planned well, but she didn't understand all that was happening behind the scenes. After another wonderful meal, the king again asked his question. "Esther, what do you want?"

Then Queen Esther answered, "If I have found favor with you, O king, and if it pleases your majesty, grant me my life—this is my petition. And spare my people—this is my request. For I and my people have been sold for destruction and slaughter and annihilation" (Esth. 7:3–4 NIV).

There comes a time in life when the ultimate question must be asked. Every batter must face the third strike, and many women are asked that life-changing question, "Will you marry me?" So Esther had planned well, and now she was ready to discuss the issue.

The king answered, "Who is he? Where is the man who has dared to do such a thing?" (Esth. 7:5 NIV).

Esther got the answer she wanted from the king, but she didn't understand how God would further work out details to completely solve the problem. When the king asked this question, all she could do was trust the hand she couldn't see, the hand of her God protecting His people.

Esther answered, "The adversary and the enemy is this vile Haman" (Esth. 7:6 NIV). Having pointed a finger at the one responsible for her death decree, and the impending death of God's people, all she could do was trust God to motivate the king to stop the slaughter.

The king was furious. Not knowing what to say, he went into the garden to cool down. Many women know what the anger of her husband means. Esther knew the king's anger was his positive response to her request. Now she had to wait patiently, as all women wait, for the unraveling of the enemy's sheet.

Haman, sensing his house of cards collapsing around him, felt his only salvation was with Esther. He rushed over and grabbed her by the ankles to plead for his life. In the agony of his request at being so emotionally upset, he didn't realize what he was doing; his hands went up Esther's legs as he pleaded more vehemently.

When the king entered the room to see Haman clutching the legs of his wife, he assumed that his prime minister was propositioning her, or at least, trying to take advantage of her.

A man's rage over anyone violating his wife is just as great as his rage at being humiliated. To humiliate a man is the destruction of his comfort and satisfaction. But to take sexual advantage of his wife is a sin against his manhood and pride. Haman had struck at the very heart of King Ahasuerus.

"Will he even molest the queen while she is with me in the house?" (Esth. 7:8 NIV). It was not a question King Ahasuerus wanted answered; it was a question of anger. But one of the servants standing by—one who was usually silent—knew the answer. This servant didn't realize the answer was from God, but those who clean our houses and serve our meals know much more of what happens in the house than their masters think they know. "A gallows seventy-five feet high stands by Haman's house. He had it made for Mordecai, who spoke up to help the king" (Esth. 7:9 NIV).

The servants must have liked Mordecai; they knew that he had saved the life of the king. They knew that Mordecai was honored by the king, and the servants must have known about the spectacle of Haman leading the king's mule throughout the city, singing the praises of Mordecai.

The Persian kingdom was ruled by the laws of the Medes and Persians. Because the kingdoms of the Medes and Persians ruled together and they didn't trust each other, they never reversed any law that was made by both. That way, one side of the kingdom couldn't take advantage of the other. The practical implication was that the law was still in effect that said anyone could still murder a Jew and keep those Jews' property. But Esther, with the practical gift of exhortation, stepped forward. She proposed a new law—her practical answer to the problem—a law that declared the Jews could defend themselves when attacked, and that they could huddle together on that appointed day to defend themselves, for there was strength in numbers and unity. If any unsuccessfully attacked the Jews to take their possessions, the Jews could reverse the action and keep the possessions of their attackers.

PRACTICAL TAKE-AWAYS

The following questions were written for group discussion with a Sunday school class or Bible study. These questions are written in the first person to help you personalize your answers and apply them to your life.

1. *Do I have the gift of exhortation?* When the Bible commands that we exhort each other daily" (Heb. 3:13; 10:25), God expects all believers to exercise the gift of exhortation in both positive and practical ways. Therefore, God expects you to be an exhorter of other people. Also, because the source of your spiritual giftedness is the Holy Spirit, you have some giftedness in exhortation. This means you have some giftedness encouraging others in a positive and practical way.

2. *Can I grow my gift of exhortation*? You can grow any gift because the Bible exhorts "stir up the gift of God" (2 Tim. 1:6); therefore, you can become more positive and practical in approaching problems in life. Any woman can grow her gift of exhortation, just as Paul told young Timothy to grow his gift of exhortation, "Give attention…to exhortation" (1 Tim. 4:13). Then Paul said, "Put these abilities to work; throw yourself into your task, so that everyone may notice your improvement and progress" (1 Tim. 4:15 TLB).

3. *Because I have the gift of encouragement, do I need someone to encourage me*? The answer is yes. While Esther had the ability to be positive and practical, she didn't act until Mordecai fasted in sackcloth and ashes outside her palace. Her cousin Mordecai motivated her to action. The motivator needed motivation. In the same way, you may have the gift of encouragement, but you might be reluctant to use it. Notice what the Bible described, "If you have any word of exhortation for the people, say on" (Acts 13:15).

4. *Do others have the gift of exhortation the same as I?* Yes, but until this century people didn't give attention to spiritual gifts, nor did they study them. Because of ignorance, many people didn't grow their gifts. Historically, in certain denominations, the gift of exhortation was also an office or position of exhortation. As a first step towards ordination in some denominations, a person received a license to exhort. This person was called "an exhorter," and possessed what is called an "exhorter's license." In some circles today, when a person preaches or speaks to a congregation, they are described as "exhorting the people."

There are many illustrations in the Bible of encouragement/exhortation in action. "Judas and Silas . . . exhorted and strengthened the brethren with many words" (Acts 15:32). Notice that this encouragement strengthened those who listened. Encouragement made people better.

In the Scriptures, Barnabas was called "Son of Encouragement" (Acts 4:36 NIV). The original King James used the phrase, "the son of consolation." This meant that Barnabas was probably a motivating speaker, one who could move people to action. When Barnabas went to give leadership to the church in Antioch, he recognized a need in the people. They needed more than exhortation, they also needed to learn and know the Word of God.

Previously, Barnabas had helped a young man (Paul) with the gift of teaching, so he went to get Paul to help teach the believers at Antioch. Notice how the Bible describes their joint ministry. Barnabas "encouraged them all" (Acts 11:23). Then, Barnabas sought Paul and together they "taught a great many people" (Acts 11:26).

WATCHING FOR THE GIFT OF EXHORTATION IN YOUNG GIRLS

1. They are happy, optimistic, and they laugh a lot.

2. They seem never to complain about things.

3. They look on the positive or "bright" side of most things.

4. They make a lot of plans (optimistic) about the future and what they are going to do.

5. They seem to have faith to trust God to work out things in their life.

6. They think in practical terms or ways to get things done.

The woman with the gift of exhortation is both positive and practical. She stimulates faith in others and gets excited about helping others live by biblical principles. She may use her gift in counseling one-on-one, or she may use it in public ministry. However she uses her gift of exhortation, others are helped practically and they are motivated to live for God.

THREE-STEP BIBLE STUDY

Step One, read the questions to get you thinking about God's name.

Step Two, analyze the verses with each question to see what the Bible says about the question.

Step Three, write your answers in the space provided.

1. Who has the gift of exhortation?

"We have been given different spiritual gifts according to the grace of God . . . if you have the gift of exhortation, then use the gift of exhortation" (Rom. 12:6, 8, author's paraphrase).

_____

_____

2. How does the gift of exhortation work in your life?

The word exhortation in Greek is parakaieo, *"to call aside, appeal to, to help, to instruct." In the dictionary exhortation means "conveying urgent advice or recommendation."*

_____

_____

3. **What is the result of exhortation and how has this been used in your life?**

"We have different gifts, according to the grace given to us . . . if it is encouraging, let him encourage" (Rom. 12:8 NIV).

_____

_____

_____

4. **How can the biblical use of exhortation work?**

"Judas and Silas . . . exhorted and strengthened the brethren with many words" (Acts 15:32).

_____

_____

_____

5. **How does this biblical command to exhort work in your life?**

"Not forsaking the assembling of ourselves together . . . but exhorting one another, and so much the more as you see the Day approaching" (Heb. 10:25).

_____

_____

_____

6. **Who is exhorted to use the gift of exhortation?**

"Exhort one another daily" (Heb. 3:13).

_____

_____

7. **Can you grow your ability to be positive and practical? Paul told Timothy, "Stir up the gift of God" (2 Tim. 1:6).**

"Give attention...to exhortation" (1 Tim. 4:13).

_____

_____

_____

8. **Do people with the gift of exhortation need encouragement to use their gift?**

"If you have any words of exhortation for the people, say on" (Acts 13:15).

_____

_____

_____

YOUR TURN TO PRAY

Add the following requests to your daily prayer list. As you pray about developing the gift of exhortation, you will find several things happening in your life: (1) Prayer gives you a desire to use your gift; (2) prayer gives you wisdom to use your gift (James 1:5); (3) prayer influences the lives of those you touch in ministry; (4) God answers by growing your gift; and (5) you grow to maturity in Christ and become more effective in use of all gifts.

1. To be an exhorter, you must be a positive person. You will not help others to practical Christianity with negative motivation. Neither will others respond to you if you are a negative person. *Lord, help me see any "critical" spirit in my heart; forgive me for being critical and negative. Give me a pure heart that loves people and has an honest desire to help others.*

2. Yield your attitudes and opinions to God. Ask Him to fill your emptiness with a positive approach to God. *Lord, I want to be a positive person—help me reach that goal.*

3. You must be practical before you can exhort others to be more practical. Ask God to help you see more practical ways you can live for Him. *Lord, I want to be an effective Christian; help me see practical ways to serve You, then help me to apply them to my life.*

4. Ask God to show you how to share practical things with others in a positive way. *Lord, may I become more positive in helping others. May I help them practice their Christianity daily.*

5. Pray for someone you know who has a negative critical spirit. Perhaps there is some way you could help that person become more positive. As you help that person, you will develop your gift of exhortation. *Lord, I pray for _____ to be more positive and practical. As You help them, help me also.*

6. Pray about places (or jobs) in the church where you could use your gift of exhortation. *Lord, I give myself to You for service; lead me to a place where I can use my gift of exhortation.*

7. Your personal prayer list:

_____

_____

_____

_____

_____

_____

_____

_____

_____

_____

_____

JOURNALING AND MEDITATION

As you study this workbook, think about the things you are learning by writing them down. You will clarify your thoughts as you express them in words. Journaling turns feelings into acts and helps you understand what's happening internally. Actually, your journal—like a diary—is like a mirror that helps you look into your soul.

1. Write a description of the most positive person you know. What do you like about that person? What does he or she accomplish with a positive attitude? What can you learn from him or her?

2. Next, think about the most practical Christian you know. Write down the things you like about that person. What can you learn from him/her?

3. Meditate on the ways you have motivated people. How have you done it? How was it effective? What did it accomplish? How could you improve your ability to motivate other people?

4. What would it take for you to become more positive in life? Write down some things you would have to do to be more positive. Make this a matter of prayer.

5. Is there a particular person you tend to be "short" with? If you are irritated with this person, how do you show it? What should you do to be more positive with that person?

6. Do you have a negative attitude toward a particular person, task, or situation? Try to analyze why you have this negative attitude. If you understand your feelings, could you change your negative attitude? Make this a matter of prayer.

7. What journaling can look like:

Day One

As the older teach the younger, a one-on-one approach can be a deeper and sometimes more lasting teaching experience.

As a young girl, I admired the beauty of my cousin's personality. I did not know terms like "role model" or "mentor," but she became an example to me of Christian womanhood. Mary Ellen is now and has always been a great influence on me, although she probably never knew it.

People watch our lives as I watched hers, and I trust someone will learn from me the positive characteristics of a Christian woman. (Ruth)

Day Two

I read "Goofus and Gallant" in the Highlights for Children magazine in the dentist or doctor's office. Goofus always made poor decisions, but Gallant was always careful to consider others or make good *character choices. Exhorters influence people without preaching or shouting. Maybe the example of others, whether written or observed in real life, can exhort us to good life principles.*

8. Now your turn to journal:

_____

_____

_____

_____

_____

_____

_____

_____

_____

_____

_____

_____

_____

_____

_____

_____

_____

_____

_____

_____

_____

_____

_____

_____

LYDIA USED HER MONEY FOR GOD'S WORK

THE SPIRITUAL GIFT OF GIVING

Carol, a petite blonde forty-three-year-old woman, never expected her husband to die of a heart attack in his late fifties. The doctor had warned them that he had a bad heart. He needed to lose weight, exercise more, and watch his diet. But he—a hardheaded businessman driven to make money—didn't listen to the doctor. He was not selfish with his money. As a deacon in the church he more than tithed, and contributed liberally to projects sponsored by the church. He always wanted to give more money and make more money. As a matter of fact, he enjoyed making money through a construction company, a realty company, and was the silent owner of three other industries in town. In addition to that, he speculated in "penny" stocks of new businesses getting started. He simply wrote off his taxes the cost of those that failed. Those businesses that made it made him extremely wealthy.

Carol's husband died needlessly of a heart attack, doing a job he shouldn't have done. After concrete finishers had smoothed out the cement floor for a new condo and left, a sudden thunderstorm threatened the newly poured concrete. Carol and her husband quickly drove over to the construction site, and he wrestled with the heavy tarpaulin by himself, trying to get the concrete floor covered before the rain destroyed it. As Carol sat in the car waiting for her husband to finish, she saw him collapse into the wet concrete. He died before the ambulance arrived. He died trying to save a few dollars invested in a load of concrete.

Now Carol has downsized her lifestyle and lives in a modest condominium, and by worldly standards, she is financially set for life. She is an excellent manager and has the spiritual gift of giving. She wrote down on a legal pad five financial goals: (1) not to make more money, but to carefully manage what she had for the glory of God; (2) to assist financially needy young people studying for the ministry, helping them through college or seminary; (3) not to give away money to "freeloaders" as her husband did, but to be sensitive to truly needy people by setting up a counseling program and teaching center to help retrain them to take care of themselves financially; (4) to continue tithing from the interest on her investments and the profits drawn from her businesses; and (5) to volunteer her time to work with a rescue mission to develop a program for women who are street people, because the mission presently only works with men.

WHAT IS THE GIFT OF GIVING?

The woman with this gift: (1) has the ability to organize her personal life to acquire money; (2) perceives individuals and places where her money is needed; (3) is sensitive to what could be accomplished by her money; (4) has a desire to give quietly and secretly so God will get the glory; (5) has faith that God will use her investments; (6) grows as she gives; and (7) becomes a positive role model to motivate others.

UNDERSTANDING THE GIFT OF GIVING

Every believer should have the spiritual gift of giving, because God expects everyone to give his or her time, talents, and treasures for His work. But God uniquely gifts certain women so that they use their spiritual gift of giving unselfishly to advance the work of the kingdom.

If you have the spiritual gift of giving, what should be your attitude in giving? The Bible describes, "Having then gifts differing according to the grace that is given to us . . . he [she] who gives, with liberality" (Rom. 12:6, 8). This verse tells us to give with simplicity, which in the original language means guilelessness. We are to give without strings or to give without a hidden agenda. When we give to God, we should not expect recognition in return.

WATCHING FOR THE GIFT OF GIVING IN YOUNG GIRLS

1. They are unselfish with their money or possessions.

2. They share their toys and things with friends at school and play.

3. They are willing to share clothes and jewelry with their sisters.

4. They are concerned about special financial projects mentioned at church and are willing to give to them, along with giving a continuing offering to God each week.

5. They manage their time and money well, being careful to not waste their money.

6. They are good shoppers, knowing how to get the most for their money. They do not spend money impetuously or frivolously, but usually do a good job of finding and purchasing what is on their shopping list.

7. They are aware of the needs (financially and physically) of their family and friends, and want to help meet these needs when able.

What do we usually associate with the gift of giving? The answer is obviously *money*. The Living Bible translates it like this, "If God has given you money, be generous in helping others with it" (Rom. 12:8).

When you have this gift, what should be your focus in using it? The NIV focuses on the purpose of giving money to God. "If it is contributing to the needs of others, let him [her] give generously" (Rom. 12:8). This tells us to give for others, implying that we don't give to get something in return, whether that is a reputation (pride) or to be placed on powerful church committees (leverage).

LYDIA HAD THE SPIRITUAL GIFT OF GIVING

"Now a certain woman named Lydia heard us. She was a seller of purple from the city of Thyatira, who worshiped God. The Lord opened her heart to heed the things spoken by Paul. And when she and her household were baptized, she begged us, saying, 'If you have judged me to be faithful to the Lord, come to my house and stay.' So she persuaded us" (Acts 16:14–15).

Lydia was a businesswoman who moved to Philippi from Thyatira, a city located in Asia Minor, today called Turkey. Apparently, in her hometown she became a seller of purple cloth because Thyatira was famous for a deep purple dye. Thyatira was a highway town on the border between the provinces of Lydia and Mysia. Perhaps she got her name from her home country of Lydia. She had probably learned to dye cloth a deep "Turkey red" from the dye of the madder-root that grew in and around Thyatira. But by the sovereign hand of God and the fate of business circumstances, she moved to Philippi. In the ancient world people didn't have the modern chemical technology to establish consistency in dying. Perhaps she moved to get a business advantage, i.e., a richer and better dye. Philippi was famous for a purple dye that came from the murex, a shellfish found in the Ganges River that flowed about a mile from the city.

We don't know if Lydia was a widow whose husband developed the business or if she was the driving force behind its development. We don't even know if she ever married, since a husband is never mentioned. But the Bible does mention she owned a large estate and had many servants. Her house was large enough to accommodate Paul, Luke, Silas, and Timothy. She probably had an estate with a large courtyard, since it was probably there the church at Philippi gathered for their services.

Perhaps getting her purple dye from the Ganges River brought Lydia back to the river on the Sabbath day for prayer. Or perhaps it was the beautiful pastoral setting that draws people there for picnics in the present day. Nevertheless, it was at this riverside that her life was changed.

What is the first characteristic of a woman who possesses the gift of giving? She must have a heart for God just as Lydia did. When Paul and his followers went out of the city to pray by the riverside, they knew it was the place where "prayer was customarily made" (Acts 16:13). They knew some were probably praying in this spot on the Sabbath day.

But it was more than prayer that qualified Lydia for the spiritual gift of giving. She had a driving desire to know God. "Lydia . . . worshiped God" (Acts 16:14). Both at the riverside and probably in her estate villa, Lydia had a heart to worship and know God.

> God was not looking for rich women to give Him money.
> God was first looking for a woman to worship Him.

Jesus told another woman about the necessity of giving God praise, "The Father is seeking such to worship Him" (John 4:23). The thing that God wants from a woman, more than money or anything else, is her worship.

After a woman worships God, what happens next? Through worship, God wants to change the focus of her life. God wants to move in her heart, completely cast out all idols, sinful desires, and pride. God wants to sweep the house clean, getting rid of impurities and her worship of false gods. This happened to Lydia as it must happen to other women, "Lydia . . . whose heart the Lord opened" (Acts 16:14).

What was the first response of Lydia to God? "Lydia . . . opened her heart to heed the things spoken by Paul. And…she and her household were baptized" (Acts 16:14–15). God wants obedience, long before He wants people's money. What good to God is a person's money, if He doesn't have her heart?

The early church leaders understood the *principle of first reference* as they studied people and doctrine. The mighty oak tree lives in the seed, long before it grows out of the ground, so a person's first response to God is a seed that shows how she will serve God later in life.

Lydia's first response as a believer reflected this principle of her spiritual gift of giving. "When she and the members of her household were baptized, she invited us to her home, 'If you consider me a believer in the Lord,' she said, 'come and stay at my house.' And she persuaded us" (Acts 16:15 NIV). The first thing Lydia did with her life after being baptized was to make her resources available for kingdom use. She took Paul and his companions into her estate and gave them free room and board so they might go about the work of the kingdom.

While the first evidence of the spiritual gift of giving might have involved some money—daily meals for four people—it probably involved the use of all her resources and reputation. But probably her greatest gift was the donation of her time. Having four men in the house probably took her time, as well as the time of her servants. As evidence of being a giver, Lydia contributed to the expanding program of God.

What evidence was there of continued giving? The church at Philippi met in Lydia's house. After Paul and Silas were released from prison, the Bible says, "They went out of the prison and entered the house of Lydia; and when they had seen the brethren [the church], they encouraged them and departed" (Acts 16:40). Two things this passage tells about the church in Philippi. First, there were brethren in Lydia's house waiting for Paul and Silas, implying more than just a few ladies were waiting to find out what would happen to Paul in jail. Lydia's leadership had attracted men to this young church. Second, when Paul got there he exhorted them, preaching a sermon to the young church that met in Lydia's house.

What was the long-term result of Lydia's spiritual gift? When Paul was in prison in Rome, he was permitted to rent an apartment for his personal use and his Roman guard. This endeavor not only involved rent, but meals and other expenses. Obviously, the Roman government didn't pay for these expenses, so the Philippian church stepped forward. "On my way, leaving Macedonia, only you Philippians became my partners in giving and receiving. No other church did this" (Phil. 4:15 TLB). The spiritual gift of a woman had been so greatly used of God that now her gift became the dominant spiritual gift of the Philippian church. Through this church Lydia continued to use her financial influence to preach the gospel through Paul.

But as we read between the lines of Philippians, we see another evidence of Lydia's spiritual giftedness. She must have given quietly and privately, for we see no evidence of Paul naming her in Philippians. He gives credit to the entire church for the money, not to Lydia. This is how a church should support a foreign missionary, not giving credit to any one person who gives a substantial share of the missionary budget; it is the church that supports missionaries.

Also, when Paul writes to the Philippians, he has to correct two ladies, "I implore Euodia and I implore Syntyche to be of the same mind in the Lord" (Phil. 4:2). It is obvious these two ladies were misbehaving in the church. While there is no hint that Lydia ever used her money wrongly, she didn't have to be corrected either. She gave as others who have the spiritual gift of giving: She gave secretly and silently. God honored her sacrifice to provide for the needs of Paul so he could write the great epistles and lay the foundations for all of us today.

HOW THE GIFT OF GIVING WORKS

She gives extra money to a new church building, sends money regularly to missionaries, supports relatives and others in Christian colleges, and donates needed equipment to missionary causes. She supports soul-winning projects, gives food to shut-ins or the needy, and gives time to nursing homes. She gives clothes to church projects, and donates time and energy to give financial advice to young couples. She counsels young business people, helps young single moms, teaches children how to save and make money, and serves on boards and fund-raising committees.

PRACTICAL TAKE-AWAYS

The following questions were written for group discussion with a Sunday school class or Bible study. These questions are written in the first person to help you personalize your answers and apply them to your life.

1. *Do I have the spiritual gift of giving?* Technically, all believers are commanded to give, not out of their abundance, but from a heart responding in love to Jesus Christ. Every believer—including you—should give money to God. First, God asks us to tithe, "Bring all the tithes into the storehouse" (Mal. 3:10). Above that, God both commands and promises, "Give, and it will be given to you" (Luke 6:38). Since we must all give, we should allow the Holy Spirit to lay projects on our hearts and tell us how much to give, as well as motivate us to give with the right attitude. However, giving involves more than money; you should give God your time, talents, and treasures.

2. *How can I become a good steward?* Your gift of giving is wrapped up in your total approach to stewardship, which is "properly managing your time, talent, and treasures for the glory of God." Notice from this definition that stewardship is more than giving money to God. It involves management of your assets, which means you must properly use everything you have—including your money—to the glory of God. Many believers are still caught up in the rat race of making and spending money. They act as if all their money, except their tithe, belongs to them. No! Everything you have belongs to God and He expects you to use it for His purpose. But many Christians still try to buy happiness or security; they still look to money as a panacea for their problems.

Winning the lottery or getting a big financial gift will not help a young couple get out of debt, even though it will give them a quick fix. They are in debt or financial bondage because they don't know how to manage the money they have. The wrong attitudes that originally got them into debt will eventually get them back into debt after the quick fix is over. Their problem is financial bondage to money. A young couple in financial bondage does not need money to solve their money problems. They need to change their attitudes about making, using, and spending money. When they change their attitude about money, they ultimately will change their bottom line.

ADVICE TO THOSE IN FINANCIAL DIFFICULTIES

1. Recognize all your money belongs to God.

2. Yield all money and possessions to Him.

3. Give your tithe and gifts to God first.

4. Pay your bills according to priority and necessity.

5. Spend less than you take in.

6. Eliminate non-essentials and luxuries.

7. Put away some for emergencies and retirement.

8. Spend all money to the glory of God.

3. *How can I grow my gift of giving?* Many women want to give more money to God, but they can barely pay their bills now. They shouldn't take away rent money for church projects. Nor should they take away money for gas or food for mission work. The following principles should guide your giving and will help you grow in stewardship.

4. *Dedicate all your money to God.* When you give a tithe, it doesn't mean that you give God ten percent and spend the remaining ninety percent as you desire. No! You must start by dedicating all your money to God, to spend it as He sees fit, i.e., spending it according to biblical principles. When you dedicate all your money to God, you then spend the remaining ninety percent according to the following prescription:

PRIORITIES IN SPENDING

1. Church obligation: Tithe

2. Life necessities: Rent, food, clothing, etc.

3. Job necessities: Transportation, insurance, business clothes, etc.

4. Family necessities: Education, health care, maintenance, and protection.

5. Home necessities: Furniture, appliances, utensils, etc.

6. Protection: Life insurance, accident insurance, disability, etc.

7. Enrichment: Personal education, travel, etc.

8. Non-essentials: Entertainment, vacations, etc.

5. *Your first act with each paycheck should be your tithe.* "Honor the Lord with your possessions / And with the firstfruits of all your increase" (Prov. 3:9). When you obey this command, God promises, "So your barns will be filled with plenty" (Prov. 3:10).

6. *Let the Spirit lead you in giving.* Since giving is a spiritual gift, the important thing in growing this gift is to let the Holy Spirit guide your giving. When you are in the center of God's will, you will grow in every area of life, including the gift of giving.

7. *How can I develop a right attitude toward giving?* There are many women with marginal or limited income. Some very poor women have an excellent attitude toward giving, but on the other hand, some have difficulty giving to God or others because they believe they don't have enough money to meet their needs. (But, then again, some wealthy women have the money, but are selfish and stingy). The first step in changing your attitude about giving is to look at the example of the Lord Jesus. "For you know the grace of our Lord Jesus Christ, that though He was rich, yet for your sakes He became poor, that you through His poverty might become rich" (2 Cor. 8:9). Next, remember that as you give with the right attitude, you will grow in spiritual giftedness. "He who sows sparingly will also reap sparingly, and he who sows bountifully will also reap bountifully" (2 Cor. 9:6). When the Bible says, "God loves a cheerful giver" (2 Cor. 9:7), it is talking about attitude. A cheerful giver is a hilarious giver—one who gives with joy, not grudgingly.

WEAKNESSES OR DANGERS OF THE GIFT OF GIVING

She (1) gives out of pride, (2) gives to control, (3) measures others' spirituality by their checkbooks, (4) may over-emphasize financial aspects of the kingdom, (5) is perceived as selfish by the people, and (6) is insensitive to people who don't manage money well.

Some think that a selfish person can't develop the gift of giving. However, study Zaccheus, a man who lied and stole to become extremely wealthy through graft and corruption. As a hated tax collector, he did what today is called "skimming." As an embezzler skims profit off the top of a corporation's income, Zaccheus skimmed his salary off the taxes he collected. Yet, when he met Jesus Christ, he was changed. "Zaccheus stood and said . . . 'Look, Lord, I give half of my goods to the poor; and if I have taken anything from anyone by false accusation, I restore fourfold'" (Luke 19:8). Just as Zaccheus was transformed into an unselfish giver, so any stingy woman clutching her money bags can be changed by God. She can develop the spiritual gift of giving.

THREE-STEP BIBLE STUDY

Step One, read the questions to get you thinking about God's name.

Step Two, analyze the verses with each question to see what the Bible says about the question.

Step Three, write your answers in the space provided.

We all know women who are unselfish and giving. But those who share their time, talent, and treasures for the kingdom have the spiritual gift of giving.

1. **If you have this gift, what should be your attitude in giving?**

    "Having then gifts differing according to the grace that is given to us . . . he [she] who gives, with liberality" (Rom. 12:6, 8).

    _____

    _____

2. **What is God saying to you about this spiritual gift?**

    "If God has given you money, be generous in helping others with it" (Rom. 12:8 TLB).

    _____

    _____

    _____

3. **But the gift of giving involves more than money. What is the focus of this spiritual gift? Remember stewardship is the proper management of time, talent, and treasures for the glory of God.**

    "If it is contributing to the needs of others, let him [her] give generously" (Rom. 12:8 NIV).

    _____

    _____

    _____

4. **Who should have the gift of giving?**

    "Give, and it will be given to you" (Luke 6:38). "'Bring all the tithes into the storehouse, / That there may be food in My house, / And try Me now in this,' / Says the Lord of hosts, / If I will not open for you the windows of heaven / And pour out for you such blessing / That there will not be room enough to receive it" (Mal. 3:10).

    _____

    _____

    _____

5. **How can you grow in your gift of giving?**

    "Honor the Lord with your possessions, / And with the firstfruits of all your increase; / So your barns will be filled with plenty, / And your vats will overflow with new wine" (Prov. 3:9–10).

    _____

    _____

    _____

6. **What does this verse tell you about growing your spiritual giftedness?**

   "He who sows sparingly will also reap sparingly, and he who sows bountifully will also reap bountifully" (2 Cor. 9:6).

   _____

   _____

   _____

7. **How can a selfish person develop this gift as Zaccheus did?**

   "Zaccheus stood and said . . . 'Look, Lord, I give half of my goods to the poor; and if I have taken anything from anyone by false accusation, I restore fourfold" (Luke 19:8).

   _____

   _____

   _____

YOUR TIME TO PRAY

Add the following requests to your daily prayer list. As you pray about developing the gift of giving, you will find several things happening in your life: (1) Prayer gives you a desire to use your gift; (2) prayer gives you wisdom to use your gift (James 1:5); (3) prayer influences the lives of those you touch in ministry; (4) God answers by growing your gift; and (5) you grow to maturity in Christ and become more effective in use of all gifts.

1. Ask God to take away any selfishness you have about your time, talent, or treasure. *Lord, I yield everything I have to you—my money, my possessions, and my schedule.*

2. Ask God to teach you priorities in life. *Lord, I have so many things to do. Give me wisdom to know what to do first and strength to do it; then teach me how to put everything else in order.*

3. Ask God to give you a "sharing" spirit. *Lord, take away my selfishness and help me learn to share with others.*

4. Ask God to make you a better manager. *Lord, there are so many things I must do and there are other things I want to do but can't. Help me keep everything straight, and help me do the right thing in the right order.*

5. Ask God to make you a better shopper. *Lord, I have to shop for necessary things and I don't get enough opportunities to shop for fun. Help me be careful with the money I have to get the best items at the best price.*

6. Ask God to help you become more aware of the material and financial needs of others and show you how you can help meet their needs. *Lord, open my eyes to someone I can help with money or in another material way, then give me wisdom how to do it.*

7. Your personal prayer list:

   _____

   _____

_____

_____

_____

_____

_____

_____

_____

JOURNALING AND MEDITATION

As you study this workbook, think about the things you are learning by writing them down. You will clarify your thoughts as you express them in words. Journaling turns feelings into acts and helps you understand what's happening internally. Actually, your journal—like a diary—is like a mirror that helps you look into your soul.

1. Think back to a gift (material or financial) you received that helped you spiritually. Write out why was it given. How did it change you? What did it do for you spiritually? Why did the person give it to you?

2. Make a list of the three greatest financial needs in your life. Pray about them. How can God be glorified when these needs are met?

3. Make a list of three things you want (not necessarily needs or requirements). How can God be glorified by your receiving these things? Make these a matter of prayer.

4. Think of one person who has a financial need. How necessary is it for this need to be met? Write out your feelings about their need. What are you going to do about it?

5. If you have financial problems, make a list of your indebtedness. Separate your debts into (a) monthly bills, (b) credit card bills, (c) large lump-sum bills, and (d) others. Pray over these bills because your testimony as a believer is tied to the way you handle these debts.

6. Think about all the financial gifts you've given to individuals and organizations. What single gift did the most good? Was it given with prayer and dedication to God? Ask God to help you do the same thing again, i.e., to bless someone else financially.

7. What journaling looks like:

Day One

    My mother was a gracious hostess, definitely ministering through her gift of hospitality. I'm sure our family entertained "angels unaware." We brought home World War II soldiers who visited our church, missionary speakers, leaders from Christian organizations, and dignitaries from foreign countries. We were just a middle-class family, but we were rich in experience. There was always an abundance of food and room for anyone who needed a home away from home. Entertaining was natural for my mother. She loved it; she thrived on it. I learned that as you exercise your gifts, you find great personal joy and satisfaction. Lord, make this gift grow in me so my family will become rich in experience. (Ruth)

Day Two

I came from a poor family, but I never realized we were poor because we had more food on our table and better food than any of my buddies; and they came from families with more money. Mother had the largest vegetable garden on our side of town, and at times my mother, brother, and sister worked in the county cannery for free cans of vegetables. I was never afraid of a boogie man under my bed because there was no room for him — over a hundred cans of butter beans were stored there.

My mother gave out of her poverty. She constantly took beans, tomatoes, and corn to the people at church, and she always cooked five or six vegetables for each meal. There were always four or five buddies playing with me in the yard. When Mother called me to eat, she'd always add, "You boys want to come watch Elmer eat?" They always answered, "Yes, ma'am," knowing they'd get a plate of food and iced tea. As Mother gave to those boys, her greatest joy was seeing them eat everything she cooked, then "Thank you, ma'am," as we went back out to play.

Lord, I don't have much to share with others, but I will give what I have. (Elmer)

8. Now, your turn to journal:

_____

_____

_____

_____

_____

_____

MARTHA WAS EFFICIENT

THE SPIRITUAL GIFT OF
ADMINISTRATION

CHAPTER

6

Linda, a middle-aged woman who manages an office for the city government, had been elected Sunday school superintendent last Friday evening. Now, it is Sunday morning and Linda, dressed in a dark suit and wearing sunglasses to protect herself from early morning glare, is on her way to church to face her new responsibility. She'll arrive early because that's the way she is. They told Linda that attendance had been declining the last three years, and that there were several problems in the Sunday school; but the board of Christian education was sure she could solve them with her administrative skills. They mentioned that some classes needed teachers, and that dates had not been scheduled for the annual Sunday school promotion, Christmas play, and spring picnic. As a matter of fact, nothing was done on the entire calendar for the coming year.

Late last evening was the first time Linda had a chance to give thought to the Sunday school, because she carefully lays out each week in an appointment book. Linda had reviewed the known problems, but she also planned to make a list of the unknown problems when she first walked through the facilities the following morning. She spent Saturday evening getting the "big picture" of her job. She read the job description in the church manual, then looked up the duties of a Sunday school superintendent in the *Successful Sunday School and Teacher's Guidebook*. Linda knew she was dealing with a sick body, just like when her children are sick. She needed a diagnosis of the problems before she could come up with medicine to make the Sunday school healthy. Before going to sleep Saturday evening, Linda tried to glance through each of the teachers' roll books, looking for trends in attendance and offerings, but she was looking especially for patterns of faithfulness in the teachers. The last thing she noted was the lack of any Sunday school training or teachers' meetings in the past year. She thought to herself, "This Sunday school has been limping along without direction, enthusiasm, or leadership."

As she prayed that Saturday evening, Linda first committed herself to the Lord, and second she asked God to give her supernatural help to turn around the Sunday school. Then, she prayed briefly for each of her workers before going to sleep.

As she arrived for Sunday school, several problems hit her in the face so quickly that she couldn't even walk through the classes to survey their weaknesses. "Mrs. Jones won't be here. What are we going to do with her class?" "The fluorescent lights are out in our classroom," a young boy said next. "Who's gonna fix them?" Then when teachers kept asking for their class roll books, Linda realized that the secretary hadn't shown up. In all, Linda needed to recruit three last-minute teachers.

"This will never happen again," Linda promised herself.

In the next week, Linda began solving the problems one at a time: recruiting new teachers, replacing burned-out lights (more than just in that one fifth-grade classroom), meeting with the Sunday school secretary, and she began working on the yearly planning calendar.

Linda is a "slot person:" She likes everything in the right place. Working with the Sunday school secretary, they cleaned up the Sunday school office, arranging all the manuals, handwork, and stationery supplies in neat stacks. Then, while working on the year's planning calendar, she studied the past year's calendar, so as not to forget to include any of the activities of the past.

For the first couple of weeks on the job, Linda was faced with unexpected emergencies, such as other teachers who didn't show up or were late. Patiently, she used "stop gap" measures to solve each pressing crisis, knowing that eventually she would have these problems in hand, and she could make future plans.

At the first Sunday school staff meeting, Linda listed the problems she saw, but she did not emphasize the negatives; she discussed policies that she felt could solve the problems. The former Sunday school superintendent had the spiritual gift of prophecy and tended to fuss or criticize when things went wrong. She got angry with teachers when they didn't show up, and her way of solving the problems was to chew out absent teachers, letting them know how much they had failed God.

Linda's approach was different; she put together a plan for substitute teachers to step in at the last moment. Linda explained that there would be emergencies, but she had a plan. "Every departmental superintendent will phone every teacher on Sunday morning during the next three or four weeks. This way we won't have surprises." But the Sunday morning phone calls also were to share the emphasis of the day and last-minute announcements. Everyone liked Linda's idea.

Within six months the Sunday school operation was humming; teachers were showing up on time. Because Linda made Sunday school exciting, her enthusiasm "trickled down," affecting everyone. Teachers began feeling Sunday school was absolutely necessary. Because Linda cared and showed it, teachers began caring and showing it to their students. Linda went the "extra mile" to buy extra teaching resources for every class. The teachers were surprised and appreciative; nothing like that had ever been done for them before.

Two administrators had run the Sunday school. With the first woman, it was a mismatch because her spiritual giftedness of prophecy didn't help her properly run the Sunday school. When the board of Christian education matched the right gifted person—an administrator—to the position, everyone prospered.

UNDERSTANDING THE GIFT OF ADMINISTRATION

The woman with the spiritual gift of administration has the ability to plan and manage her tasks so that the work of God prospers. Paul mentions the spiritual gift of administration.

> *"We have been given spiritual gifts that differ from other believers, this gift is based on the grace that God has given to us . . . he [she] that has the gift of administration, do it with diligence"* (Rom. 12:6, 8, author's paraphrase).

WATCHING FOR THE GIFT OF ADMINISTRATION IN YOUNG GIRLS

1. They like to keep their room and things in order, and will keep things in place, whether it's toys when young or cosmetics when they reach the teens.

2. They approach homework with a sense of sequence and deliberation, doing each job in the right way.

3. They tend to be task-oriented in both play and helping around the house.

4. When they want to do several things, they have the ability to put them in order, then follow the order as they complete the tasks.

5. They like to play with more than one doll, making sure the dolls do things together.

6. They are "savers," whether they save stuffed animals, souvenirs, or they stuff things into books or scrapbooks.

7. They make good, dependable baby-sitters.

8. They can carry out instructions from parents and teachers.

What does the old word for administration mean, i.e., rule? Originally, the gift of administration was called the gift of ruling. "He [she] that ruleth, with diligence" (Rom. 12:8 KJV). Usually we think of a king or queen ruling upon a throne with absolute power. However, the word *rule* means to be a manager or a leader. The way the word *manager* is used today reflects the biblical meaning. Quite often in today's businesses, people are not called office managers, but office leaders; nor are they called sales managers, but team leaders. There is another meaning suggested by the NIV that describes this gift: "And in the church God has appointed . . . those with gifts of administration" (1 Cor. 12:28).

WHAT IS THE GIFT OF ADMINISTRATION?

A woman with the gift of administration: (1) has the ability to see the overall picture and make long-range objectives, (2) knows the task needed to complete the project, (3) is able to delegate tasks to others, (4) can counsel and motivate others to get the job done, and (5) judges others by the completed task.

What does an administrator do? Those who administer a program at the church should be willing and able to do everything that they oversee. The woman who oversees the kitchen should be able to cook, fix the salads, set the tables, and wash the dishes. However, those who are administrators also should have the "big picture" and be able to work with all the ladies so that each person gets her job done easier, quicker, and the whole job is done better, and each lady grows in Christ by serving in the kitchen.

Administrators are managers, and there are only four things that can be managed: time, people, money, and resources. Everything fits into one of these four categories.

HOW TO MANAGE

Manage time . . . with a daily schedule.

Manage money . . . with a budget.

Manage people . . . with job descriptions.

Manage resources . . . with a planning calendar.

The administrator is a "slot" person; she likes to put things in slots for efficiency. If you visit her kitchen, you find all the silverware in the appropriate drawers, glasses are together, cans of soup are separated from the cans of vegetables, and everything is in its place ready for use. When you look in the dresser drawers of her bedroom, she has all the socks matched by size and color, and they're all stacked perfectly, pointing in the same direction. The same with blouses, and her shoes are orderly in the closet.

WHAT IS A "SLOT" PERSON?

An administrator puts the right person in the right "slot" to do the right job with the right tools, in the right way, at the right time.

What is the focus of an administrator? When you read The Living Bible, you see that a woman's emphasis in administration is helping people. "Here is a list of the parts he has placed in his Church, which is his body . . . Those who can help others" (1 Cor. 12:28). Here, the purpose of an administrator is not efficiency or to save money or to save time. The biblical gift of administration helps people grow in Christ and helps the body of Christ bring glory to God. If you are gifted in administration, your passion should be to carry out the purpose of the church and bring glory to God.

What should be the attitude of the woman who administers a task in the church? Romans 12 tells us she should do her work "with diligence" (v. 8) and "take the responsibility seriously" (v. 8 TLB). This means she naturally focuses on getting tasks done. She puts things in order, knowing she is bringing unity to the body of Christ.

MARTHA, THE ADMINISTRATOR

"Now it happened as they went that He entered a certain village; and a certain woman named Martha welcomed Him into her house. And she had a sister called Mary, who also sat at Jesus' feet and heard His word. But Martha was distracted with much serving, and she approached

Him and said, 'Lord, do You not care that my sister has left me to serve alone? Therefore tell her to help me.'" And Jesus answered and said to her, 'Martha, Martha, you are worried and troubled about many things. But one thing is needed, and Mary has chosen that good part, which will not be taken away from her'" (Luke 10:38–42).

From what is written about Martha, apparently her dominant gift was administration. When given a task of planning a meal, she saw it through until the end.

What did Martha possess? The Bible says that Mary and Martha lived in "her house" (Luke 10:38), suggesting Martha was the owner of the house. Some think Martha got her house when her husband died, others think that she purchased the house because she was a good worker/businesswoman. She also was a "giver" because Martha apparently took care of her brother Lazarus and her sister Mary.

How does Martha first reflect her gift of administration? When Jesus first came to the home of Martha, the Bible says she "was worrying over the big dinner she was preparing" (Luke 10:40 TLB). She was task-oriented, and since Jesus came to her home, this probably meant His disciples plus other people in the area were coming to her house for dinner. Since Martha had to prepare a big banquet, she wanted it to be right, so she spent the afternoon cooking, setting the table, getting table decorations, making sure everything was right. A "slot" person wants everything in the right place.

What is the attitude of Martha the administrator toward others? As Martha was scurrying around the house to get everything ready, her sister Mary was sitting at the feet of Jesus. Mary was learning from Jesus. Martha, like most people with specific task gifts, gets annoyed when her tasks don't get done. Because Mary didn't share her concern, Martha got irritated at Mary. Notice her response: "Lord, do You not care that my sister has left me to serve alone?" (Luke 10:40). Martha wanted to put her sister to work to get ready for the evening meal; probably she would have put any other person to work who was there. We don't know everything that was said that afternoon. Perhaps Martha had previously asked her sister to help, but Mary ignored her. So Martha said to Jesus, "Therefore tell her to help me" (Luke 10:40).

WEAKNESSES OR DANGERS OF THE GIFT OF ADMINISTRATION

She (1) appears insensitive to the needs of individuals, (2) becomes power-hungry, (3) uses people to get a job done, i.e., manipulation, (4) lowers her Christian standards to get the job done, (5) becomes a bureaucrat, or (6) complains when things are not organized.

What two things concerned Jesus about Martha? Jesus was called upon to mediate a problem between two women, two sisters. All of us know that a woman might hold her tongue when irritated with another woman in the church, but one sister speaks plainly to another sister. When Jesus was called to mediate the problem, He said, "Martha, Martha, you are careful, but agitated about many things" (Luke 10:41, author's paraphrase). Jesus had two observations about Martha. First she was "careful." This means she was given to details to make sure they got done, and in this observation, Jesus identifies Martha as an administrator because she was driven by details. But Jesus had a second observation: Martha was "troubled." This word *turbazomia* means "to be agitated." When Martha came to Jesus, her voice was sharp and her face showed irritation. Jesus—who knew people perfectly—knew the heart of Martha.

How did Jesus solve the problem? Even though Jesus pointed out two things about Martha, He was concerned about only one. He said, "But one thing is needed" (Luke 10:42). Jesus probably meant it was all right for her to be careful about details in preparing the meal. But the second thing was not acceptable, i.e., Martha shouldn't be irritated. In another story when Jesus comes to raise Martha's brother from the dead, again Martha shows irritation at the Lord. "Lord, if you had been here, my brother would not have died" (John 11:21).

WHAT AN ADMINISTRATOR EXPECTS

She expects others will help, because she is task-oriented.
She expects others to be responsible, because she cares.

What other spiritual gift often goes with administration? Martha not only could delegate jobs to other people; she also had the gift of serving or helps. "Martha was distracted with much serving" (Luke 10:44).

Did Jesus mean Mary was better than Martha? After Jesus told Martha not to be irritated, He told her, "Mary has chosen that good part, which will not be taken away from her" (Luke 10:42). Jesus did not make a comparison, saying that Mary was better than Martha. What Jesus suggested was that looking after details was all right, but she should be committed to the right purpose for administering details. Martha was focused on planning a meal, but Jesus and His ministry should have been her focus. The Living Bible explains the purpose of Jesus when He said, "There is really only one thing worth being concerned about. Mary has discovered it—and I won't take it away from her!" (Luke 10:42).

WHAT THE GIFT OF ADMINISTRATION DOES

She is a Sunday school administrator, homemaker, office manager, president/owner of a company, teacher, administrative assistant, personnel director, choir director, and PTF officer. She organizes church dinners, plans VBS, arranges church mailing lists, supervises a cleaning detail, and plans children's parties. She begins a speaker's bureau for women speakers.

Women with the gift of administration must remember that they are organizing a task so that the work of Christ is done for His glory. Some women have felt a clean kitchen was the only reason why a church kitchen committee exists. They have forgotten the focus of service to the body of Christ.

PRACTICAL TAKE-AWAYS

The following questions were written for group discussion with a Sunday school class or Bible study. These questions are written in the first person to help you personalize your answers and apply them to your life.

1. *Do I have the gift of administration?* Because we are all made in the image of God, and God runs all things "decently and orderly," we should allow God to express His orderly nature in our daily lives. All of us have some degree of giftedness in administration. On a scale of 1-10, some women keep house like a 2 and other women are a 10. The women with the 2 may feel that the family relationships in a house are more important than keeping every utensil in perfect order. However, even those who prize relationships should bring some order to their home and some organization to their family. The Bible teaches, "everything should be done in a fitting and orderly way" (1 Cor. 14:40 NIV).

2. *What can I do if I'm not organized?* There are some women who are so interested in relationships, they only clean their house when they have to. Other women feel a clean house reflects a clean soul and a clean purpose in life. Still other women feel a house should be comfortable. Rather than saying, "I just can't get organized" or "I don't like housework," every woman can grow in her organizing ability. It's not a matter of what you like, it's a matter of what God wants you to do and how He is glorified in your home. No matter what your spiritual gift, you can grow in your management ability. This means you can become a better organized person, and you can administer your family in a better way. The key is desire—what do you want to do? The Bible tells us, "Earnestly desire the best gifts" (1 Cor. 12:31). If you want to be a better administrator, God will help you grow that ability.

THREE-STEP BIBLE STUDY

Step One, read the questions to get you thinking about God's name.

Step Two, analyze the verses with each question to see what the Bible says about the question.

Step Three, write your answers in the space provided.

1. **What does the word *rule* mean?**

    "Having then gifts differing according to the grace that is given to us . . . he [she] that ruleth, with diligence" (Rom. 12:6, 8 KJV).

    _____

    _____

    _____

2. **What is the meaning of the word *administration* used in the NIV to describe this gift?**

    "And in the church God has appointed . . . those with gifts of administration" (1 Cor. 12:28).

    _____

    _____

    _____

3. **What kind of skills or abilities should an administrator have?**

Administrators put the right person in the right place to do the right job with the right tools at the right time for the right purpose.

_____

_____

_____

4. **What is the emphasis of the gift of an administrator found in The Living Bible?**

"Here is a list of some of the parts he has placed in his Church, which is his body . . . Those who can help others" (1 Cor. 12:28).

_____

_____

_____

5. **What attitude are we to take when administering our gifts?**

"Having then gifts differing according to the grace that is given to us . . . he [she] that ruleth, with diligence" (Rom. 12:6, 8 KJV). "Take the responsibility seriously" (Rom. 12:8 TLB).

_____

_____

_____

6. **Martha had the gift of administration, but she also had another gift that she used. How do these gifts go together?**

"Martha was distracted with much serving" (Luke 10:40).

_____

_____

_____

7. **What is the ultimate purpose of the diligent administrator?**

"There is really only one thing worth being concerned about [knowing Jesus]... Mary has discovered it—and I won't take it away from her!" (Luke 10:42 TLB).

_____

_____

_____

8. **How should we exercise the gift of administration?**

"Everything should be done in a fitting and orderly way" (1 Cor. 14:40 NIV).

_____

_____

_____

9. What can be said to the woman who is disorganized?

> *"Eagerly desire the greater gifts"* (1 Cor. 12:31 NIV).

_____

_____

_____

YOUR TIME TO PRAY

Add the following requests to your daily prayer list. As you pray about developing the gift of administration, you will find several things happening in your life: (1) Prayer gives you a desire to use your gift; (2) prayer gives you wisdom to use your gift (James 1:5); (3) prayer influences the lives of those you touch in ministry; (4) God answers by growing your gift; and (5) you grow to maturity in Christ and become more effective in use of all gifts.

1. If you are not very organized, ask God to give you a mentor to guide you so you can manage better. *Lord, give me a friendly helping hand so I can get better organized.*

2. Ask God to give you a passion to be better organized. *Lord, give me a desire to take control of circumstances and give me wisdom how to do it.*

3. Some feel guilty because they are not better organized and the more they see their weakness, the worse they feel. Ask God to forgive your failure, to show you positive things to get better organized, and give you the stamina to go get it done. *Lord, forgive me where I failed, show me what to do, and give me passion to put things in order.*

4. Some women have a hard time getting organized because their children are too young, or their family is too large, or their husband works at home or they have to work one or two jobs. *Lord, I can barely hang on, much less get better. Help me to do the necessary, and when I let things go, take away my guilt.*

5. Pray for God to help you become more task-oriented. *Lord, give me discipline to finish the jobs I start.*

6. Pray for grace to help you handle interruptions and "time-wasters." *Lord, help me look at my things to do as You see them. Help me to work as steadily as You would, then help me handle interruptions as You would.*

7. Your personal prayer list:

_____

_____

_____

_____

_____

_____

_____

JOURNALING AND MEDITATION

As you study this workbook, think about the things you are learning by writing them down. You will clarify your thoughts as you express them in words. Journaling turns feelings into acts and helps you understand what's happening internally. Actually, your journal—like a diary—is like a mirror that helps you look into your soul.

1. Make a list of the tasks you have to do tomorrow that are over and above your normal duties. Now stop and pray about the list. Ask for God's help. Next, put your tasks in priority of importance. Again, pray and ask God if any of these duties can be erased from the list. Look at the list again, separate the tasks into those that can be done quickly and those that need time. After you've made the list, promise yourself you'll work diligently on them in their proper order.

2. If you're not organized, write the name of a woman you admire who is a good manager. Why is she good? Write what it is about her that you admire. What about her could you first adopt?

3. If you were a better manager, what ministry at church would appeal to you? Why would you like to serve in that way?

4. Write yourself a letter requesting that you become the administrator of the _____ (you fill in a ministry) at church. How could you best be approached to persuade you to volunteer? What strengths could you bring to that ministry?

5. Suppose you had a title such as personnel director at your church and you had to coordinate all the volunteers. How would you approach the job? What would you do to get more people to volunteer? If your church has a hard time getting volunteers, how would you approach the task differently?

6. What journaling can look like:

Day One

When I (Ruth) became director of Family Life Services, an adoption agency, I realized that I needed help with my administrative duties, so I began each Monday morning with a staff meeting. We had a time of prayer and each staff member would discuss her agenda for the week. We readjusted, gave advice, added or changed duties, and I came away from the meeting with an organized weekly calendar.

Daily planners, calendars, lists, PalmPilots, and computers are great organizational tools. As an administrator, I required each staff member to use some kind of organizational tool.

Day Two

"People don't do what you expect; they do what you inspect!"

As an administrator, I needed to learn to use my staff according to their spiritual gifts. I never had to remind the office manager to order more 3x5 cards or paper for the printer. She was good at details.

Our secretary kept me informed of daily appointments and calls to answer, while Jill was always the one with whom I discussed reports for a board meeting or a new policy we needed to adopt. (Ruth)

7. Now, your turn to journal:

_____

_____

_____

_____

_____

_____

_____

_____

_____

_____

_____

_____

_____

_____

_____

_____

_____

_____

_____

_____

_____

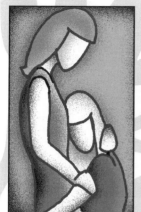

NAOMI COUNSELED HER DAUGHTER-IN-LAW

THE SPIRITUAL GIFT OF
MERCY-SHOWING

Janie, a freckle-faced young mother whose skinny body and youthful zeal make her appear to be much younger than she is, and whose infectious smile makes her seem less spiritual than she is, in reality has the spiritual gift of mercy-showing or counseling. When Janie and her husband were watching their favorite TV game show, the phone rang. She took the call, but went in the other room when the voice on the other end was crying. Her husband complained, "Have her call back. You'll miss your favorite program." But Janie was on the line for two hours because a woman with the gift of mercy-showing will sacrifice to exercise her gift.

Janie is an executive assistant to the president of a new growing .com company. Her boss hired Janie because she had strong gifts in administration, and he has raised her pay several times because he says, "When I make a decision, she makes it happen." Janie is a whiz at delivering messages to department heads; she never gets the message wrong, and the department heads always get it right.

But what Janie's boss doesn't realize is the other major contributive role Janie makes to the progress of the company. When a decision is needed urgently and he can't call his board of directors or his department heads, he talks through the decision with Janie. She listens, she affirms, and she helps him think through the problems and various decisions. Janie is the boss's sounding board. He sees the problem through Janie's eyes—then makes his decision. Janie's natural talent is counseling; her spiritual giftedness is mercy-showing.

Because of her reputation of helping other young struggling wives through problems, the pastor has recommended Janie as a church counselor. The church provides an office, and one night each week, she talks to three young women—one hour each. She's so good, the husbands ask to come with the wives when they see progress in their homes.

The church has asked Janie to come on as a full-time counselor, or at least part-time. Her boss won't hear of it. He put through a raise for her company stock options.

UNDERSTANDING THE GIFT OF MERCY-SHOWING

A woman who has the spiritual gift of showing mercy will empathize and sympathize with individuals or groups who have problems and conflicts. When she sympathizes, she feels *for* their problems; when she empathizes, she feels *with* their problems. By relating to hurting people, she identifies with their problems and helps them put things back together. She will show them God's mercy and give them support as they work their way back to wholeness.

WHAT IS THE GIFT OF MERCY-SHOWING?

A woman who has the gift of mercy-showing has the ability to: (1) empathize with hurting people, (2) form a relationship to support them in time of need, (3) communicate God's acceptance to them, (4) use her faith to lift them up, and (5) help people to wholeness because of her great belief in them and God.

What is the greatest contribution of a mercy-shower? A woman who is helping another is not just primarily showing her kindness to them; she is showing the mercy of God to them. Therefore, in her counseling relationship she is communicating God to a needy person. Remember God is "the Father of mercies, and God of all comfort" (2 Cor. 1:3). Therefore, a mercy-shower is simply a channel through which God communicates His comfort to hurting people.

What does the gift of mercy-showing tell us about the woman who has it? To be a mercy shower, a woman must know God and spend time with God; the bottom line is she must be godly. When the Bible says, "The Lord is full of compassion and mercy" (James 5:11 NIV), He depends upon His servants to communicate His compassion and mercy to those who need it.

How is God's mercy first communicated to a mercy-shower? Technically, mercy begins with salvation, "according to His mercy He saved us" (Titus 3:5). No one deserves salvation; God in mercy gives us His love and forgiveness. Therefore, the woman who is a mercy- shower has first experienced God's mercy in salvation. Then, she passes God's mercy on to those who need it.

WATCHING FOR THE GIFT OF MERCY-SHOWING IN YOUNG GIRLS

1. They tend to be sensitive when they see others suffer and want to do something for the hurting person.
2. They tend not to argue with brothers, sisters, or friends.
3. They love to sit and listen to older adults.
4. They are very sensitive to babies when baby-sitting.
5. When their playmates fuss, they tend to be peacemakers.
6. They tend to obey the directions of adults quickly.
7. They tend to be listeners, rather than talkers, not taking the limelight.
8. They will notice when another child is left out or is overlooked, and they want all of their friends to be treated fairly.

What kind of people will the mercy-shower usually help? Obviously, the woman who is a mercy-shower will focus her ministry on hurting people, because God "will have mercy on His afflicted" (Is. 49:13). Again, the Bible says, "Hear, O LORD, and have mercy on me; / LORD, be my helper!" (Ps. 30:10). Look how many times in Scripture people cried out to Jesus, "be merciful to me . . ." The woman who is a mercy-shower will want to spend time with those who need her, i.e., those who are hurting, discouraged, broken, or imprisoned in habits.

When you show someone God's mercy, you are communicating God's presence to him or her. The mercy-shower opens up the heart of God. In the Old Testament, God's presence dwelt in the Tabernacle in the Holy of Holies on the ark of the covenant. The lid on the ark (the word *ark* meant box) was called a mercy seat. God does not have an earthly throne; rather He sat upon the mercy seat. Just as a husband will sit on a cedar chest at the foot of a bed to change his shoes (the ark of the covenant was about this size), so the box upon which God sat had the name *mercy*. "I will appear in the [*shekinah*] cloud upon the mercy seat" (Lev. 16:2 KJV). Therefore, to be effective in showing mercy, a woman will want to get close to God and know Him. To be an intercessor for the needs of others, she will come into the presence of God to find mercy for others.

What is foundational to showing mercy to others? The woman who has this gift is naturally good at relationships. She not only likes people, she gets along well with them. Whereas the woman with the gift of prophecy may irritate people because she upholds the honor of God against sin, and the woman with the gift of administration puts people to work, the mercy-shower touches their lives and becomes their friend. "All have different gifts according to the grace that is given to them . . . if it is the gift of showing mercy, let her do it cheerfully" (Rom. 12:6, 8 author's paraphrase). The Living Bible puts it this way: "Those who offer comfort to the sorrowing should do so with Christian cheer" (Rom.12:8).

Who has the gift of showing mercy? Let's not just think that God gave a few women the gift of showing mercy and counseling. Technically, every believer should be grateful that the mercy of God has extended to her, and every believer should extend that mercy to others. Jesus said, "Blessed are the merciful, for they will be shown mercy" (Matt. 5:7 NIV). So every believer reading this book has some giftedness in showing mercy.

How does the mercy-shower measure her gift? Those with the gift of teaching measure their gift by how much their students learn, and the servant measures her gift by how she serves others. The administrator measures her gift by accomplishing tasks. What about the mercy-shower? She measures her effectiveness in small deeds of mercy. Did not Jesus say, "Whoever gives one of these little ones only a cup of cold water. . . assuredly, I say to you, he shall by no means lose his reward" (Matt. 10:42)?

WHAT A MERCY-SHOWER DOES

She visits the sick and shut-ins, counsels those with problems, listens to those who hurt, takes meals to families who have lost a loved one, gives time to those who need it, sits with the dying, helps in hospitals and rest homes. She baby-sits for others, listens to problems over coffee, prays with those who have grief, is sensitive to people who are discouraged. She listens to those who think about quitting, gives time to the poor, and helps at the rescue mission.

> ## WEAKNESSES OR DANGERS OF THE GIFT OF MERCY-SHOWING
>
> She (1) offers help when it is not wanted, (2) becomes too intimate with other's lives, i.e., becomes a busybody, (3) attracts people to herself who are problem people, (4) lacks firmness in dealing with issues and truth, (5) can base Christianity on emotions and feelings, and (6) resents those in the church who do not have the compassion that she has.

What other way describes a mercy-shower? She shows mercy by sharing her life with others. The very nature of sharing is seen in the traditional definition of mercy: Mercy is the goodness of God manifested toward those who are in distress. So a mercy-shower is really sharing God's mercy with hurting people. She does this by listening to problems, because God is concerned about our problems. She sympathizes/empathizes with problems because God feels the anguish of our problems. She directs people to solutions and answers because God wants us to be victorious over our problems. She rejoices when others take a step toward wholeness, because that is God's desire for them.

Just because a woman has the gift of showing mercy doesn't mean she can become all things to all people. There are some who need a rebuke from God, but rebuke comes from the prophet. Others need teaching from the teacher, and in certain situations the administrator must step in to organize a number of women to get a task done in the church.

NAOMI, THE MERCY-SHOWER

Whereas most women have a large dose of mercy, and several women in the Bible were mercy-showers, perhaps Naomi is the most characteristic mercy-shower. Naomi gave support to her daughter-in-law Ruth at a crucial time so that Ruth made the right decision to follow God. At other times, Naomi gave Ruth wise counsel that solved crucial problems in her life. Both women prospered because of Naomi's wisdom.

The problem began in the Book of Ruth when Naomi's husband made a wrong decision to leave Bethlehem in the promised land to move to Moab, a heathen country. Naomi manifested her passive nature as mercy-shower by going along with her husband rather than arguing with him or refusing to go. There is no record in the Scriptures that Naomi attempted to stop him. "There was a famine . . . And a certain man of Bethlehem, Judah, went to dwell in the country of Moab, he and his wife and his two sons" (Ruth 1:1). Those who have visited the town of Bethlehem remember that it's located in the high Judean hill country. Moab can be seen from Bethlehem. When the famine dried up their fields, Naomi and her husband could look out across the Jordan Valley some twenty miles away to see the green fields of Moab. Naomi's husband chose by the physical eye—not the heart—and moved his family to live in Moab—out of the promised land. While it was not a sin to leave the promised land, Naomi's husband did not trust God to take care of him and his family in times of need. He did not remain in the center of God's will. So he and his wife left the security of home and friends to move to a foreign culture, taking their two sons with them.

What did they lose beside their walk with God? Once they arrived in the land, the two sons married outside their faith, marrying Moabite girls. Naomi's husband was the first to pass away, and then both of Naomi's sons passed away, leaving Naomi in a foreign land. Living in a foreign culture without her husband and sons, all Naomi had left were her two daughters-in-law.

Even though discouraged, Naomi knew she had to return home. She told her daughters-in-law goodbye and left Moab to return to Bethlehem. Orpah stayed in Moab, but Ruth, her other daughter-in-law, insisted on coming with Naomi to Bethlehem. When Naomi got home, she told her family and friends, "Do not call me Naomi; call me Mara [means bitter], for the Almighty has dealt very bitterly with me" (Ruth 1:20).

Naomi's mercy-showing became apparent when Ruth wanted to go work with the servants in the field. God had commanded the owners of farms to allow the poor to glean grain that was left in the field by harvesters. This was Israel's equivalent to welfare work. We see a picture of Naomi listening to her daughter-in-law, then giving her good counsel. Naomi "said to her, 'Go my daughter'" (Ruth 2:2).

That day in the fields, Ruth worked hard and caught the attention of the owner, Boaz. Being a wise owner, he told his servants to let Ruth glean the fields right behind them, and if she wanted some water from the jar that was provided for his workers, he told them to let her have a drink.

When Ruth brought home more grain than most gleaners, Naomi reacted wisely, knowing that Ruth had some help. "So much!" Naomi exclaimed. "Where in the world did you glean today? Praise the Lord for whoever was so kind to you" (Ruth 2:19 TLB). A good counselor knows when to ask questions, knows what questions to ask, and knows that answers will lead to further insight. Naomi knew that Ruth couldn't have gathered all the grain without help. When she heard the story of how the owner of the field had been kind to her, Naomi correctly counseled, "God has continued his kindness to us as well as to your dead husband! Why, that man is one of our closest relatives!" (Ruth 2:20 TLB).

After the harvest was finished, Naomi knew what would happen. She knew that the men would gather in the evening to thresh the grain when the cool winds began to blow. After the kernels were separated from the chaff, and divided into different piles, the men would sit down to eat, and then sleep by their grain to guard it throughout the night. Naomi knew that timing was important, and that a great decision depended on timing. So she counseled Ruth, "Now do what I tell you—bathe and put on some perfume and some nice clothes . . . but don't let him [Boaz] see you until he has finished his supper" (Ruth 3:3 TLB).

What happened is a picture of Asian custom. After Boaz went to sleep, Ruth laid down to sleep at his feet—not illicit sex as some suggest—she slept crossways at his feet. Ruth slept as a servant would position herself to the master for protection or service. Boaz awakened in the night, realizing someone was there. It was then that Ruth asked him to be the kinsman redeemer of the estate of her dead husband. Ruth applied the Asian analogy saying, "I am Ruth, thy handmaiden, spread your blanket over your handmaiden, for you are a family redeemer" (Ruth 3:9, author's paraphrase). Obviously, involved in her request was his marriage to her. We always think of the man asking the young lady for marriage, but here was a biblical account of the young lady setting the stage for marriage. (He chased her until she caught him.) Perhaps Ruth wouldn't have been so bold without the counsel and encouragement of Naomi.

Boaz promised that he would become the redeemer of her bankrupt estate, but there was one relative closer in line than he. Boaz said he would take care of it the next day and sent Ruth home with a large supply of grain.

When Ruth got home, again Naomi was ready to counsel her. Whether Ruth was anxious or discouraged is not known. But the wise counsel of Naomi knew what to say. "Just be patient until we hear what happens, for Boaz won't rest until he has followed through on this. He'll settle it today" (Ruth 3:18 TLB).

> Naomi knew Ruth.
> Naomi knew the man.
> Naomi knew when to act.
> Naomi knew when to wait.

The next morning Boaz went to the gate at the city, the place where business was conducted. He met the man who was closer in family relationship to Ruth, and challenged him to redeem Ruth's estate out of bankruptcy. When the man revealed that he had other marriage plans, Boaz then paid the redemption price and bought Ruth and her husband's estate out of bankruptcy. They married, and as wonderful stories go, they lived happily ever after.

Now what about Naomi the counselor? What did she get for her counseling? Sometimes counselors charge by the hour and receive a fee. In church ministries when counselors have been very effective in helping others, sometimes they are given a gift. Naomi's gift was seeing her daughter-in-law married, and eventually she got to see her grandson, Obed. "Naomi took care of the baby, and the neighbor women said, 'Now at last Naomi has a son again'" (Ruth 4:16 TLB).

PRACTICAL TAKE-AWAYS

The following questions were written for group discussion with a Sunday school class or Bible study. These questions are written in the first person to help you personalize your answers and apply them to your life.

1. *Can I ask God to increase my gift of mercy-showing?* Suppose you don't think you are a very good mercy-shower. What can you do about it? The Bible tells us that you can ask for wisdom (James 1:5) and God will give you wisdom. But wisdom is not merely facts written on paper, or knowledge apart from life. Nor is wisdom merely information we read in the encyclopedia. When God gives us wisdom, He gives us Himself with His wisdom. Therefore, when you are asking for mercy, you get to know the person of God. "The wisdom that is from above is . . . full of mercy" (James 3:17).

2. *Can I become more sensitive?* As you study the nature of God in the Bible, it will make you more godly, or more like God. Because God is sensitive to people, you'll become more sensitive to people as you become more intimate with Him.

Also, praying for people will make you more sensitive to them. As you pray for the specific needs of specific people, you will want to help them in tangible ways, as well as support them emotionally. Usually, the gift of mercy-showing goes hand in hand with the burden of prayer intercession of others.

THREE-STEP BIBLE STUDY

Step One, read the questions to get you thinking about God's name.

Step Two, analyze the verses with each question to see what the Bible says about the question.

Step Three, write your answers in the space provided.

1. **What should be your attitude toward showing mercy to others?**

    "We have different gifts, according to the grace given us . . . if it is showing mercy, let him [her] do it cheerfully" (Rom. 12:6, 8 NIV). "Those who offer comfort to the sorrowing should do it with Christian cheer" (Rom. 12:8 TLB).

    _____

    _____

    _____

2. **Where does the gift of mercy-showing come from? What can be said about the giver of this gift?**

    "The Lord is full of compassion and mercy" (James 5:11 NIV). "The Father of mercies, and God of all comfort" (2 Cor. 1:3).

    _____

    _____

    _____

3. **What must you have to be a mercy-shower?**

    "Blessed are the merciful, for they will be shown mercy" (Matt. 5:7 NIV).

    _____

    _____

    _____

4. **In what ways has God prepared you to be a mercy-shower?**

    "According to His mercy He saved us" (Titus 3:5).

    _____

    _____

    _____

5. **The Bible tells us God will show His mercy on what kind of people? Look up the word *mercy* in a concordance, then study how people asked Jesus, "Be merciful to me . . ."**

    "Will have mercy on His afflicted" (Is. 49:13). "Hear, O LORD, and have mercy on me; / LORD, be my helper" (Ps. 30:10).

    _____

    _____

6. **List some of the small ways we can show mercy to needy people.**

    "Whoever gives one of these little ones only a cup of cold water...assuredly, I say to you, he shall by no means lose his reward" (Matt. 10:42).

    _____

    _____

7. **If we don't have mercy, for what should we pray?**

> *"If any of you lacks wisdom, let him ask of God, who gives to all liberally and without reproach, and it will be given him" (James 1:5). "But the wisdom that is from above is first pure, then peaceable, gentle, willing to yield, full of mercy and good fruits, without partiality and without hypocrisy" (James 3:17, emphasis added).*

_____

_____

_____

8. **How close do you come to the standards of a mercy-shower?**

A mercy-shower has the ability to: (1) empathize with hurting people, (2) form a relationship to support them in time of need, (3) communicate that God will lead them to wholeness and His acceptance of them, (4) use her faith to lift them, and (5) have great belief in people.

_____

_____

_____

YOUR TIME TO PRAY

Add the following requests to your daily prayer list. As you pray about developing the gift of mercy-showing, you will find several things happening in your life: (1) Prayer gives you a desire to use your gift; (2) prayer gives you wisdom to use your gift (James 1:5); (3) prayer influences the lives of those you touch in ministry; (4) God answers by growing your gift; and (5) you grow to maturity in Christ and become more effective in use of all gifts.

1. Pray for the needs of those to whom you minister. As you pray for them, your sensitivity for them will grow. You then will want to support them emotionally and help them through counseling. *Lord, give me eyes to see the real needs of others so I can properly pray for them.*

2. Ask God to show Himself to you so you can be more godly. *Lord, show Yourself to me, so I can show Your mercy to others.*

3. Pray for opportunities to share your heart with those who need counseling. *Lord, open the door for me to help one person who needs encouragement and support.*

4. Pray that you become a better counselor and friend to needy people. *Lord, give me a greater heart for needy people and allow me to help them.*

5. Ask God to develop your ability to listen to others so you can better understand and help their needs. *Lord, give me a patient heart to listen to others and give me a sensitive heart so I can understand what I am hearing.*

6. Ask God to help you develop counseling skills to better help others. *Lord, I want to grow as a person and become a better counselor. Give me a heart that is able to support and help others.*

7. Your personal prayer list:

_____

_____

_____

_____

_____

JOURNALING AND MEDITATION

As you study this workbook, think about the things you are learning by writing them down. You will clarify your thoughts as you express them in words. Journaling turns feelings into acts and helps you understand what's happening internally. Actually, your journal—like a diary—is like a mirror that helps you look into your soul.

1. Make a list of several people who you think are needy. Begin praying for them, asking God to show their inner needs to you. Then ask God to give you opportunities to help them. As you pray for them, begin writing in your journal how you will listen to them and what you will do to help them.

2. Was your mother a good listener? A good counselor? Write down the things that made her a good mercy-shower.

3. Look around your church to find a good female role model who is showing mercy. Write down the things she does well. What are her motives and what are her rewards?

4. There have been times when you have listened to a friend, or you helped support someone in need. Write down your feelings when you used your gift of mercy-showing. Is this your strongest gift? How will you use this gift in the future?

5. There are many reasons in our modern world why some women do not have an opportunity to take time to listen or counsel others. Some have action-oriented jobs in which they can't talk because they are kept busy. Others find themselves busy with several children, and still others have long commutes to work. Make a list of the barriers that keep you from giving time to needy people. Now write an answer to the following: How can I give some time to at least one needy person? Is my "busyness" evidence that I don't want to give time to others?

6. Let's face it, some women are not socially driven; they don't like to talk or listen. They have other dominant gifts and they serve God in other ways. If this is you, write a reflection of your gifts and how you can best serve God.

7. What journaling can look like:

Day One

Some of the "predictions" in my high school yearbook were accurate. It said I would be a helper of people. When I went back for my fiftieth reunion, the committee helped us remember each other by using our yearbook pictures as identification badges. Few of us were really recognizable; our physical features had changed over the years. But our personalities were much the same. Our class president was still in a leadership mode and his skills were recognized in his vocation as well.

One of my old friends approached me with the question, "Do you remember me?" She was still slim and pretty, friendly and full of energy. She went on to ask, "Remember our after-school conversations? I still refer to them today when I make important decisions. You helped me so much!"

I didn't remember any of the content, only her friendship. As we review the past, we sometimes gain insight into our "budding" abilities. These are our spiritual abilities that God develops in us over the years and uses the rest of our lives. I didn't realize that I was counseling during those after-school meetings, but it was meaningful to my friend even fifty years later. Today I realize my dominant spiritual gift is counseling. (Ruth)

8. Now, your turn to journal:

_____

_____

_____

_____

_____

_____

_____

_____

_____

_____

_____

_____

_____

_____

_____

_____

_____

DEBORAH HAD A MESSAGE FROM GOD

THE SPIRITUAL GIFT OF
PROPHECY

CHAPTER

8

Lucille turned to her husband as they drove home from church, remarking, "The ladies' dresses are shorter this summer than ever before." Her husband didn't say anything, so Lucille continued, "One lady had on a sundress that revealed too much cleavage." Lucille was concerned about the temptation to sexual fantasies by men in the congregation. Her stylish suit had matching buttons high around the neck and on the sleeves. She was the picture of conservative dress.

Turning to her two children in the back seat, she said, "Go straight to your room and take off your church clothes . . . and don't forget to hang them in the closet. They have to be clean for tonight."

That afternoon Lucille would go to the corner of Elm and Main to parade for the Right to Life March; she felt that it was important that America put an end to abortions.

Lucille's gift of prophecy reveals itself in small ways. At the dinner table she gave a series of commands to her son: "Don't talk with your mouth full, take your elbows off the table, you can't leave the table until you're excused." She was not mad, nor was she punishing him, it's just that Lucille wanted her son to act right when he grew up. Because of her watch-care, Lucille had the best-behaved children in church; the other ladies often complimented her on her children's obedience.

Lucille became passionately motivated to do something about sex on the Internet when her young son asked an innocent question. "What's a condom for?" Up until that point, Lucille couldn't even turn on a computer. Because of the potential harm to her children, Lucille took an introductory class to use the computer, and learned to surf the Internet. When she saw the vast opportunities for children to surf into sexually explicit Web sites, she became furious. It was then that she found out that a Christian-oriented provider had an automatic block against sexually explicit sites. Immediately, Lucille signed up for it, and dropped the service the family was using. Lucille then went on a crusade at church to let other families know about the potential damage to their children. She got the pastor to make announcements about the problem, then distributed application forms for church members to sign up for the family-friendly network provider.

Next, Lucille wrote her senators, congressmen, and the president of the United States to complain about pornography on the Internet. When they wrote back to her about "free speech," she fired off a letter in response telling them that no one had the freedom to destroy young lives with filthy speech.

Lucille wrote letters to the editor to warn other people about the dangers of pornography on the Internet, and when the license was to be renewed by the city council for the cable providers, she went to the council meeting to voice her complaints about X-rated films on the movie channels. She was not ashamed to tell them, "Sex is a beautiful thing given by God. Why should we let filthy entrepreneurs ruin our families?"

Because Lucille is self-motivated, she was interviewed on the local six o'clock news during the community profile slot, where she warned other mothers about sexual problems on the Internet. She gave her phone number to attract and organize others who had the same passion.

Last fall, Lucille had a display at the county fair to make families aware of the threat to their children, and next summer she plans to take her booth to the state fair.

UNDERSTANDING THE SPIRITUAL GIFT OF PROPHECY

What is the spiritual gift of prophecy? A woman with the gift of prophecy has a deep passion to defend the reputation of God and she opposes those who violate the honor of God or the standards of justice. However, not every woman has this dominant gift of prophecy. Some women are mercy-showers, which means they are sympathetic toward hurting individuals, trying to bring them to wholeness, while a woman with a prophetic gift is more concerned about the standards of right and wrong, to make sure the evil doesn't happen again. Those women with the gift of prophecy are passionate to protect their children from potential harm and corruption. Paul reminds us that some women may view ministry differently because they are gifted differently, "having then gifts differing . . . if prophecy, let us prophesy" (Rom. 12:6).

WATCHING FOR THE SPIRITUAL GIFT OF PROPHECY IN YOUNG GIRLS

1. They are careful to obey their parents and have a sense of guilt when they fail.

2. Because they have a high degree of right and wrong, they will correct or criticize their playmates for misbehavior.

3. They are sensitive to Sunday school lessons or sermons on sin.

4. They tend to be quicker to do what their mother asks.

5. When playing with others they tend to want other children to do what they are doing.

6. They normally think they are right and others are wrong when there is a disagreement about whether an action is right or wrong

7. Sometimes adults think these girls have a strong ego, when all they want is for others to do the right thing.

God gives to some women a strong commitment of what is right and wrong. When a woman warns her children not to accept rides from strangers, she may be a typical mom, but when she reports a suspicious car cruising the neighborhood, or she gets the "Neighborhood Watch" sign erected, she may be exercising the gift of prophecy. A typical mom knows that eating ice cream before dinner will spoil her child's appetite and make him sick, but the woman with the gift of prophecy may punish her children so they won't do it again. It's not that the woman prophet doesn't love her children, she expresses her love by keeping them from getting sick.

Women with the gift of prophecy passionately correct their children when they eat with their hands, teaching them to use a fork, because it's the civilized thing to do. My (Ruth) mother washed my mouth out with Fels Naphtha soap because I said a bad word. When she reached over in church to squeeze my arm, I knew that talking during the sermon was wrong. Washing out my mouth or squeezing my arm was an act of prophecy, reminding me what was right and keeping me from doing wrong.

When a mother punishes a child for coming in late from a date, or won't let him get away with a lie, she may be exercising her gift of prophecy, which means she has a strong passion for right. My (Elmer) mother, who had a definite gift of prophecy, used to tell me, "Do right and you'll be right." It was more important that I develop good character than having a good time playing.

WHAT IS THE GIFT OF PROPHECY?

A woman with the spiritual gift of prophecy: (1) passionately defends God's reputation and standards, (2) has great insight about what happens to those who compromise God's standards, (3) warns about compromise, (4) is strong and courageous to oppose those who break the law, and (5) understands the sinful motivation of people.

Does the woman with prophecy just warn against evil and corruption? It appears at first glance that women with a prophetic gift use more negative motivation than positive; they don't want their children harmed, and it seems as though they put love on the back burner. But in fact, the woman with the gift of prophecy will warn against evil because she loves her children deeply. "Everyone who prophesies speaks . . . for their strengthening, encouragement and comfort" (1 Cor. 14:3 NIV). This tells us that the prophet will build up people or strengthen them and will encourage people to do right by keeping them from doing wrong. They will help the sick by keeping them from eating or doing things that will harm them. Paul also says, "He who prophesies edifies the church" (1 Cor. 14:4 NIV) which means she will build up people by the things that she does.

Are there any human sources for the gift of prophecy? This is a question that seems to have no explainable answer. Some women have "sharp" tongues because their mothers were very blunt and demanding. But at the same time, another daughter from the same family may react to her mother, developing an opposite mild temperament, rarely, if ever, criticizing. One daughter often criticizes, the other seldom does. So where does a woman get her gift of prophecy? All we can say is that it comes from God. "And God has appointed these in the church: first apostles, second prophets . . ." (1 Cor. 12:28). After all is said and done, the gift of prophecy comes from God, but we can't always describe how He delivered it to us. Sometimes it comes from birth, at other times it comes from our family or other circumstances.

WHAT THOSE WITH THE GIFT OF PROPHECY DO

The woman with the gift of prophecy joins MADD (Mothers Against Drunk Drivers) and opposes drunkenness, gambling, abortion, prostitution, and X-rated bookstores that will corrupt children. She crusades against drugs, alcohol, and any form of wickedness. She will warn people about sexual addiction, get petitions signed, write letters to the editor, march in the annual Right to Life March, and defend the family at city hall meetings. She will do everything to keep her children from doing wrong, and she will punish them when they are wrong.

DEBORAH: JUDGES 4:1–24

Deborah, the third of the Israel's judges, is considered one of the greatest female leaders of the Old Testament. She lived with her husband, Lappidoth, on the border between the tribes of Benjamin and Ephraim. Multitudes came to Deborah to determine the will of God for their lives, or to hear the Word of God. People went to a prophet/prophetess when facing a decision or when they needed justice. They probably went to a prophet/prophetess because the high priest was not effective in counseling or godly in lifestyle. When God could not speak through the Urim and Thummin on the high priest's breastplate, God raised up a prophet/prophetess to speak to His people. This seems the case when God raised up Deborah to speak to the people.

Deborah held court under the palm tree of Deborah, probably not a tree named for her. Some think Deborah the prophetess was named after another Deborah, for whom the tree was named. Earlier in Israel's history (Gen. 24:59) a young girl was sent along with Rebekah as her servant, and later became her wet nurse. Outliving Rebekah, Deborah became attached to Jacob and Rachel's household, dying at a very great age (Gen. 35:8). She was buried under the "oak of weeping" called *Allon-Bachuth*, which became Deborah's tree, i.e., the tree named after the servant Deborah. Later there was a baby girl named Deborah, perhaps after Rachel's servant or because she was born near the tree and was named for it. This baby girl grew up to be Deborah, the one with the gift of prophecy. Many came to this Deborah so that the prophetess could interpret for them the will of God and help them make decisions.

Why was Deborah given the title prophetess? She was called a prophetess (Judg. 4:4). Some think this was her title because she was married to a prophet, Lappidoth. Those who say this might have a male-dominated view of ministry and not want to think of a woman in ministry. They would say Deborah ended up in ministry because her husband was ineffective or disqualified himself.

But the context doesn't suggest this. Lappidoth was never called a prophet, nor is there any suggestion he was involved in ministry. Deborah was called a prophetess because she could mediate the Word of God to the people who came to her and she correctly prophesied an offensive from Mount Tabor that defeated Israel's enemies.

Deborah was the third and greatest judge whose presence rallied an army. She accompanied them to battle, where her presence motivated them to victory. In our day a judge, such as Supreme Court Justice Sandra Day O'Connor, weighs evidence and makes legal decisions. During the time of the Book of Judges, judges were military leaders, political leaders, spiritual leaders, and statesmen/stateswomen. But Deborah was also called a "mother in Israel" (Judg. 5:7), revealing the tender compassion and care she gave to her people.

While Deborah was called a prophetess—a biblical term—most evangelicals do not call women prophetesses today. They refer to women as having the gift of prophecy, although it would not be wrong to call them prophetesses.

What was Deborah's main task? When the multitudes came to Deborah, the Scriptures indicate "the Israelites came to her to decide their disputes" (Judg. 4:5 TLB). That means she was much like an appointed judge who sits on the legal bench, listening to both sides of a dispute, then making a decision based on existing law. She might hear a civil case over possession of an animal, or perhaps settle a dispute in which one Israelite had damaged another. As a prophetess, Deborah did more than give her decision based on the Law; she communicated "the will of God" and what God would decide in such disputes.

What was Deborah's legal symbol of authority? It appears that Deborah didn't have a courthouse where she would make official decisions. In biblical times, legal decisions were usually made by men who "sat in the gate." Usually this was a platform near the gate to the city where official business was conducted during the daytime. The platform might be used for entertainment in the evening. Also, the platform was used when people wanted to communicate to others in the city. But Deborah, a woman without access to sitting in the gate with the men of the city, apparently conducted her court in the open country, under the palm tree of Deborah. Perhaps she used this palm tree because of the great respect and deep sentiment people had for that location. Also, she may have used this spot because she was named after the tree.

What prophetic ministry did Deborah have? In addition to making legal decisions, Deborah also made predictions about the future. She sent for Barak, apparently one of the leaders of the tribe of Naphtali, and told him, "The God of Israel commands you: 'Go, take with you ten thousand men . . . I will lure Sisera the commander of Jabin's army, with his chariots and his troops to the Kishon River and give him into your hands'" (Judg. 4:6–7 NIV).

Deborah may have felt the great oppression by the Canaanites because the people who came to her told horrible stories of violence and oppression. Perhaps many of the cases she decided were motivated by Israel's poverty because the Canaanites had invaded their land, stole crops, and siphoned off their wealth. As Deborah empathized with the people's suffering, she knew something had to be done. It was then that God gave her a word of prophecy.

What was Israel's greatest need? Previously, God had raised up Shamgar, apparently a judge who fought by himself but who killed over six hundred Philistines. Before that Ehud was the second great judge who delivered Israel out of the hands of Moab. But the people of Deborah's day faced a new threat. The Canaanites came sweeping down from the north in their iron chariots, not just to conquer Israel but to plunder and take Israel's wealth back to their great walled cities in the north.

God had given Israel over to the Canaanites because Israel disobeyed God in worshiping the idols of their heathen neighbors, intermarrying with them, and turning from strict worship of Jehovah. The Bible says, "Israel again did evil in the sight of the LORD" (Judg. 4:1). As a result, there were no great miracles for the people of Deborah's day such as the miracles that God gave Joshua when Israel conquered the land. Rather, when God's people turned their backs on the Lord, He allowed their enemies to defeat them because they turned from God: "The LORD sold them into the hand of Jabin king of Canaan . . . he has harshly oppressed the children of Israel" (Judg. 4:2, 3).

What was the response to Deborah's prophecy? Deborah told Barak that God had spoken, and Israel would be victorious over Sisera, King Jabin's commander. Like so many cases in which a woman believed God but the man doubted, Barak did not fully believe the Lord would deliver them, nor was he willing to do what Deborah said. Reading between the lines of Scripture, a scared man is seen hiding behind the skirts of a woman. Barak told Deborah, "I'll go, but only if you go with me!" (Judg. 4:8 TLB).

Women who have the gift of prophecy are not always heard by others. Why? Because other people don't always see the vision that a woman with prophecy sees. Also, they don't have her convictions and they don't want to change their lifestyles. Perhaps they are afraid of what they will lose. But in this case, Israel had little to lose. Probably any woman with the gift of prophecy will meet opposition and should be prepared to be courageous in the face of non-compliance. What child wants to be told he can't have ice cream before dinner, and what abortion clinic operator wants to shut down his business because of opposition?

What was Deborah's response when her prophecy was not fully received? Deborah had spent her ministry dealing with the will of God. When people came to find God's will, they probably obeyed. But this occasion with Barak was different. Deborah had called him; he had not come seeking prophecy—or a job—from her.

Barak had a yellow streak. He told Deborah, "If you will go with me, then I will go; but if you will not go with me, I will not go!" (Judg. 4:8). We must always be careful not to tell God, "I will not go!" That is rebellion against God. Also, be careful about dictating to God how you will do what He commands.

Perhaps Barak thought that God wouldn't speak through a woman, or maybe he thought that a woman's word shouldn't be obeyed. In those days, the role of a woman was not as respected as it is today, but that was no excuse! Inasmuch as God had been speaking through Deborah to the people who came to "Deborah's tree," it was not Deborah that Barak disobeyed. Barak was disobeying God.

When Deborah heard Barak's response, she said "Very well . . . . I will go with you. But because of the way you are going about this, the honor [credit] will not be yours, for the LORD will hand Sisera over to a woman" (Judg. 4:9 NIV).

This is what the gift of prophecy does. It warns people when they are reluctant to do God's will. Barak had refused to do what God had said, so Deborah warned him that he would win the battle, but he would not get credit for it.

How did God give the victory? The battle was fought in the Valley of Armageddon, also called the Plain of Jezreel. At the east end of the valley is a tall hill called Mount Tabor—not a mountain with steep cliffs, rather a hill with a gentle slope all the way to the top. A runner could dash from the top to the bottom, or in today's terminology, you could drive your RV all the way to the top of Mount Tabor. Israel's ten thousand soldiers camped at the top of Mount Tabor, and in the Valley of Armageddon, King Jabin rallied his army under the command of his general Sisera and their nine hundred iron chariots.

Israel was no match for iron chariots. All the Israelite warriors had were spears and bows and arrows. When Israel formed a battle line—men shoulder-to-shoulder—the Canannites' charging chariots of iron wheels would crush any human flesh in its way. Israel's army didn't stand a chance, except for God. God sent a violent rainstorm, accompanied by thunder and lightning that turned the valley floor into a bog, "The earth trembled and the sky poured down its rain" (Judg. 5:4 TLB). "The rushing Kishon River swept them away—that ancient river" (Judg. 5:21 TLB). When the valley flooded, Israel's charging army along with thunder and lightning terrified the Canaanite soldiers, and they began running in every direction. Sisera, who should have been courageously rallying his troops, also ran wildly away. In his flight, he came to the tent of Jael, a woman from the tribe of the Kenites—who were Bedouins living in tents, moving from place to place.

Sisera escaped the vicious storm by entering Jael's tent. Then asking for something to drink, she gave him milk. Being exhausted from running, he lay down to sleep. Jael covered him with a blanket, then took a tent stake and, hammer in hand, put the stake to his temple, and drove it through his head into the ground. Sisera didn't die instantly. The Bible says, "He sank, he fell" (Judg. 5:27). Apparently, he struggled and thrashed on the tent floor before dying.

The fifth chapter of Judges is Deborah's psalm of victory, considered one of the first evidences of Jewish poetry in the Bible. In this psalm, Deborah praises God for the victory by Jael. Deborah sings, "Most blessed of women be Jael . . . her hand reached for the tent peg, her right hand for the workman's hammer. She struck Sisera, she crushed his head, and she shattered and pierced his temple. At her feet, he sank, he fell; and there he lay . . . dead" (Judg. 5:24–27 NIV).

PRACTICAL TAKE-AWAYS

The following questions were written for group discussion with a Sunday school class or Bible study. These questions are written in the first person to help you personalize your answers and apply them to your life.

1. *If I have the spiritual gift of prophecy, what are some gifts that will accompany prophecy?* Usually those women who have a strong giftedness of prophecy also have a strong giftedness of evangelism. Why? Those who have such a clear view of sin also want to deal with sin in God's way. Since the only answer to sin is salvation and a new heart, women with the gift of prophecy usually have a strong passion to lead people to Christ. Since you can't lead a person to salvation until that person realizes he is lost, then the gift of prophecy will show people their sinful condition.

2. *What is my greatest danger if I have the gift of prophecy?* Those with the gift of prophecy have to be careful they don't fall into legalism. When you have such a strong passion to point out wrong, the tendency is to think that when you *do right*, you are right with God. However, just keeping the law never saved anyone and just keeping the law never made anyone a good Christian. You become an authentic Christian when you ask Jesus Christ to come into your heart. Then you live the Christian life for the right reasons when you ask the Holy Spirit to take control of your life, i.e., the Spirit makes you *spiritual*, and the Holy Spirit makes you *holy*.

WEAKNESSES OR DANGERS OF THE GIFT OF PROPHECY

Some women with the gift of prophecy (1) are so opposed to sin that many times they condemn the person who does wrong, along with condemning his sin, becoming insensitive to people; (2) can be viewed as hard and judgmental; (3) sometimes have difficulty seeing the other side of an issue or another person's point of view; (4) become dependent on a fight to keep motivated; (5) become so concerned with standards that they are no longer oriented to people who must live the standards; or (6) are motivated by pride or selfish motives.

3. *What type of motivation will I tend to use if I have the gift of prophecy?* Those with the gift of prophecy tend to motivate people negatively. Negative motivation is warning and pointing out the consequences of actions. Get a mental picture of the Old Testament prophet putting his finger in someone's face, warning him "You are the one." This is negative or condemning motivation. This person feels he/she can motivate others by warning them of the consequences of wrong actions. Obviously, there are some women who tend to be more negative than positive. They see a demon behind every bush, they see a germ on every lunch counter, and they fear pneumonia every time their child sneezes. Those women, who see more evil in the world than good, continually warn other Christians about breaking God's law. They *can* become pessimistic because they are so focused on a negative world.

4. *How will my negative motivation relate to other gifts?* Women with the gift of prophecy have to be careful of being critical of those with other gifts. A woman with the gift of prophecy may criticize someone who doesn't feed her children properly, not realizing that the other woman is a mercy-shower who feels that if her child wants ice cream . . . why not? The prophet may criticize other women who don't march at city hall, or women who don't take petitions door-to-door to close down a porno shop, not realizing those with the spiritual gift of teaching want to instruct about evil, and those with the gift of exhortation use positive motivation to get people to live practical and positive lives. In describing spiritual gifts, Paul said that the eye was not the hand, and the toe was not the ear (2 Cor. 12:14–25). Each of us, like parts of the body, contributes to the unity of the whole. God has given each woman different spiritual gifts to carry out His purpose in the body of Christ.

5. *Who is more likely to be my friend if I have the gift of prophecy?* Those with a prophetic gift usually make friends with those who also have the same gift. You will meet each other in training sessions where you'll be taught how to gather petitions, or join forces in a Right to Life March, or you'll sit next to each other at a protest meeting at city hall. It is only natural that birds of a feather flock together. But there are two steps to this process. First, a woman with a prophetic gift may have difficulty making friends because she may turn off all other women with different gifts. Because other gifted women don't join her crusade, the woman with the prophetic gift may view them as compromisers or weak Christians, or at the least, not worthy of her friendship. So, she doesn't seek out friendships with those who don't share her burden. Second, the woman with the prophetic gift tends to use negative motivation, hence alienating herself from those who use positive motivation. Others may talk behind her back, saying something like "Who wants that grouch around?"

6. What is the "flip side" of having a prophetic gift? We have already said that she is not usually positive in motivation. Another weakness of women with prophetic gifts is that they are usually fighters not builders. Because they passionately defend God's reputation by fighting evil, their priority is not the craft of a careful builder who will lay one brick upon another, or will carefully teach one Sunday school lesson after another. However, this doesn't make them any less necessary in the kingdom of God. Both types of women are needed in God's work. Jesus instructs us to be both builders and battlers. "I will build My church . . . the gates of Hades shall not prevail against it" (Matt. 16:18).

THREE-STEP BIBLE STUDY

Step One, read the questions to get you thinking about God's name.

Step Two, analyze the verses with each question to see what the Bible says about the question.

Step Three, write your answers in the space provided.

1. **Do you have the gift of prophecy? How is it reflected in your ministry?**

    "Having then gifts differing . . . if prophecy, let us prophesy" (Rom. 12:6).

    _____
    _____
    _____

2. **What does the woman with the gift of prophecy do besides warn against evil?**

    "Everyone who prophesies speaks to men for strengthening, encouragement and comfort" (1 Cor. 14:3 NIV). "He who prophesies edifies the church" (1 Cor. 14:4 NIV).

    _____
    _____
    _____

3. **Where does one with the gift of prophecy get her gift? What influenced you to develop this gift?**

    "And God has appointed... first apostles, second prophets . . ." (1 Cor. 12:28).

    _____
    _____
    _____

4. **What can the woman with the gift of prophecy do for her church?**

    "He [she] who prophesies edifies the church" (1 Cor. 14:4 NIV).

    _____
    _____
    _____

5. **How does the woman with the gift of prophecy know she is right?**

"The spirits of the prophets are subject to the prophets" (1 Cor. 14:32). "You are responsible for any prophecy you speak to make sure it is right" (1 Cor. 14:32, author's translation).

_____

_____

_____

YOUR TURN TO PRAY

Add the following requests to your daily prayer list. As you pray about developing the gift of prophecy, you will find several things happening in your life: (1) Prayer gives you a desire to use your gift; (2) prayer gives you wisdom to use your gift (James 1:5); (3) prayer influences the lives of those you touch in ministry; (4) God answers by growing your gift; and (5) you grow to maturity in Christ and become more effective in use of all gifts.

1. To grow your gift of prophecy, ask God to give you a greater sense of right and wrong. *Lord, open my eyes to Your standard of right and wrong.*

2. Because those with the gift of prophecy can become legalistic, ask God to give you pure desires to do right. *Lord, make me see right as You see it, and make me do right for the correct reasons.*

3. To make sure your motives are always right, yield yourself to the control of the Holy Spirit. *Lord, I give myself to You, may the Spirit make me spiritual and may the Holy Spirit make me holy.*

4. Pray that your family will always do the right thing with the right motive. *Lord, help me to live right so I can help my family live right.*

5. There are many evil influences that can harm your family. Ask God to help you protect them from evil. *Lord, keep my family from evil, help me to see what will harm them, and help me guide and protect them.*

6. There are many evil forces in the world; you can't fight them all. Ask God to give you wisdom to pick your battles and strength to fight them. *Lord, give me wisdom to know when to act and speak against evil and give me wisdom to make a difference.*

7. Your personal prayer list:

_____

_____

_____

_____

_____

_____

_____

JOURNALING AND MEDITATION

As you study this workbook, think about the things you are learning by writing them down. You will clarify your thoughts as you express them in words. Journaling turns feelings into acts and helps you understand what's happening internally. Actually, your journal—like a diary—is like a mirror that helps you look into your soul.

1. Make a list of the evil things that bother you or that can harm you and your family. After listing them, put them in order of priority. Now separate them into a list for prayer and a list for action. Write what you will do.

2. If you don't have a strong gift of prophecy, write your feelings about the gift. If you want to grow this gift, write why.

3. What woman do you respect who is a "crusader" for a cause? Why do you respect her? What is there about her that you would like to emulate?

4. If you had a greater spiritual gift of prophecy, against what issue would you take a stronger stand? Why did you choose that issue? What would you do?

5. The woman with the gift of prophecy tends to motivate negatively. Write how you tend to motivate. All of us motivate negatively at some time. How do you do it? When do you use negative motivation? When are you positive? Why do you use positive motivation at times?

6. What does your family need more from you—positive or negative motivation? How would you begin to change? What would you look like if you changed?

7. What journaling looks like:

Day One

> What does a negative attitude do to you?
>
> Frown lines in your forehead, sharp, hurtful tones in your voice, upset stomach, hurtful words—you make people around you miserable. You cause poor judgment and decisions, finally you remove hope. (P.S. It's all right to be negative toward sin.)
>
> RX for a cure:
>
> Keep a prayer list and check off answers—then count your blessings.
>
> Do you have physical problems that cause depression? —See a doctor.
>
> Are you a moody person affected by weather? I am.
>
> Turn lights on—play music—scrub—do something for someone else.

Realize how destructive your attitude is and if other things do not help, seek counseling.

Day Two

When I was a child, I knew better than to ask my parents if I could go to the home of one of my friends to spend the night. My mother never gave a reason, but she would suggest that I ask Jackie to stay overnight at our house instead. Jackie lived with her mother, where from time to time her "uncles" would visit. I always thought my mother just loved company, but now I see her wise protection of me. I'll always remember the night my mother led my friend Jackie to accept the Lord as Savior.

8. Now, your turn to journal:

_____
_____
_____
_____
_____
_____
_____
_____
_____
_____
_____
_____
_____
_____
_____
_____
_____
_____
_____
_____
_____

MARY MAGDALENE HAD A FOLLOWING

THE SPIRITUAL GIFT OF SHEPHERDING

Some women tend to be natural-born leaders, and Virginia is one of them. She usually walks confidently into a room as though she owns it. Other women follow her because they think she owns it. In every grade at high school, Virginia always seemed to be the center of the girls' activities. When she decided to play jump rope, her friends followed. When she decided to wear the school letters on her sweater, all the girls followed. When they discussed going to a movie, each girl had a choice, but whatever Virginia wanted to see is where they all went. Virginia was not proud, nor was she arrogant; it's just that the other girls followed her.

It was only natural that Virginia became a cheerleader, and in student government she eventually held all the offices: secretary, vice president, and in her senior year, president of the student council.

Virginia was converted to Christ through Campus Crusade in her freshman year at the university. Almost immediately, Virginia let everyone know she was a Christian. She'd go through the dormitory on Bible study nights, gathering up all her dormmates. Even those who were not interested in Bible study attended because they couldn't say no to Virginia.

Now Virginia is married and has two children in grade school, and even though she is in her early thirties, she has risen to leadership among the women of the church.

When the pastor wanted to begin an earlier worship service at 8:15 A.M., there was some resistance among the older members of the church board. An old-timer stood up to say he represented the older members, "Having two worship services will split our church." Another stood up to complain: "If we have two worship services, I won't know everyone."

When the church board finally agreed to try the early worship service, the pastor turned to Virginia to organize workers in the church lobby to greet the worshipers as they arrived. He told Virginia she might have trouble getting volunteers because of the opposition expressed by the board. Virginia shrugged off the criticisms, telling everyone that an early worship service would be a great idea to attract new people to the church. When the pastor saw her enthusiasm, he knew he had asked the right person to extend hospitality to people as they came early to church.

Virginia didn't believe all of the older people were against the idea. The first thing she did was to ask two of the elderly ladies to provide coffee and sweet rolls in the lobby for those who came early. She challenged the ladies, "Let's get here thirty minutes early and have coffee ready for our workers, the ushers, the parking lot greeters, the welcoming team, and the choir." Because the elderly ladies had the spiritual gift of serving, they rallied to the opportunity, and on the first Sunday the smell of freshly brewed coffee in the vestibule welcomed visitors out of the brisk fall mornings.

Next, Virginia asked some young couples to act as host and hostess in the front lobby. With large nametags, the "Welcoming Team" assisted the ushers in greeting people, registering them at the welcoming table, and Virginia made sure that the host and hostess memorized the names of the visitors, so they could call them by name as newcomers left the auditorium after the sermon.

Because Virginia always had a cheerful smile, she infected her team, creating an inviting atmosphere to greet people coming to the early service.

Virginia also had two other ladies act as registrars for the early service. Everyone who came to the early service got a personal handwritten note from the ladies on the welcoming committee, inviting them to return the next Sunday. But the welcoming committee went a second mile. It quickly established a list of those who were regular early morning attenders, and when they missed a service, both a phone call and letter followed to let the absent members know they were missed.

After six months in the early morning service, the pastor asked all the workers in the early service to come forward to receive a special gift in appreciation for their service . . . a rose. Virginia had arranged this to show them appreciation. In offering the flower to them, the pastor said, "This early service is responsible for thirty-five new people who have joined our church or received Christ. Reaching these people has been a joint effort of all of those who are standing before you: ushers, greeters, hospitality committee, welcoming committee, and sidewalk greeters, all of you." Even though the pastor recognized all who had made the early church service a success, most of them knew in their heart it wouldn't have happened without their leader—Virginia. Even though she was not recognized in a special way, they all knew that Virginia was the driving force that motivated them to reach the thirty-five new people in the church. Virginia has the spiritual gift of shepherding. And just as sheep naturally follow a shepherd, so the people of the church naturally follow Virginia.

UNDERSTANDING THE GIFT OF SHEPHERDING

The woman with the gift of shepherding draws others to herself, where she cares for them spiritually and leads them to follow and serve the Lord.

WHAT IS THE GIFT OF SHEPHERDING?

The woman with this gift (1) has a strong motivation to see others follow and serve Jesus, (2) has a high degree of sensitivity to the relationship of others to Jesus, (3) can oversee the equipping and employing of others to serve and follow Jesus, and (4) is concerned about the needs of individuals and the group.

If Jesus is our Shepherd, why do people need a human shepherd? People need a shepherd today, just as they did during the physical life of Jesus. "When he [Jesus] saw the crowds, he had compassion on them because they were harassed and helpless, like sheep without a shepherd" (Matt. 9:36 NIV). Because Jesus is not humanly present in the church, He has appointed people with the gift of shepherding to carry out His work. Because people are sheep who cannot take care of themselves and because they constantly open themselves up to danger and destruction, Jesus has appointed shepherds to take care of them. Because many people won't feed themselves spiritually, He has appointed shepherds to feed them. People need shepherds to guide them to spiritual health and maturity.

How could anyone take the place of Jesus? Every believer looks to Jesus Christ as his/her example because, "the LORD is my shepherd . . . He leads me" (Ps. 23:1, 3). We are all reminded that Jesus said, "I am the good shepherd" (John 10:11). Toward the end of the New Testament, Jesus still had that recognition as "that great Shepherd of the sheep" (Heb. 13:20). So, even though God gives humans the gift of shepherding, in a real sense, the only real shepherd we have is Jesus Christ.

How does Jesus shepherd His sheep through a woman? Since Jesus is our Shepherd, but He is not physically here to lead His sheep, He has gifted individuals to lead His sheep. A female shepherd does not take the place of Jesus, but she allows her Savior to lead His sheep through her. In this way, the woman with the gift of shepherding leads sheep for Jesus. And since Jesus indwells her, she allows her Lord to use her for His glory. Remember, Jesus told one of His disciples, "Feed My lambs" (John 21:15). Then He extended the command, "Tend My sheep" (John 21:16). Jesus expects us to do His work while He is in heaven, and He uses both women and men to get His work done.

What is the secret of successfully shepherding others? If you are to shepherd other people for Jesus, then you must have His love, His wisdom, and His grace. You can get this through *double transference*. Jesus said, "You in Me, and I in you" (John 14:20). This means that Jesus will come into our hearts when we are converted, because salvation is asking Jesus Christ to come into our lives. Once we have Christ in us, then we allow His love, wisdom, and grace to flow through us to other people. But there is a second part to double transference. More than having Jesus in our hearts, we are perfect in Him. As the Lord Jesus sits at the right hand of God the Father, when we become Christians, we are placed "in Christ" and we have God's fullness because we are perfect in Christ.

WATCHING FOR THE SHEPHERDING GIFT IN YOUNG GIRLS

1. They usually make a decision about what games their friends will play.
2. They are looked to by their friends for answers and decisions.
3. Teachers usually choose them to lead in projects because they take charge in other class activities.
4. They have positive ego strengths and are self-assured.
5. They size up situations before other children, then know what decision or action is needed.
6. They are usually outgoing and make friends easily.
7. They have been pushed into leadership roles because of other outstanding traits, such as good grades, athletic ability, or a natural talent like singing, etc.

What is another name for the gift of shepherding? The New Testament does not specifically identify a "gift of leadership." Technically, the authors feel that all women have some leadership ability, and they lead through the various spiritual gifts that have been given to them. The teacher leads through her teaching, the exhorter leads through her practical and positive exhortation. The woman with the gift of administration leads others by her managing ability. The woman who has the gift of shepherding leads by spiritual oversight. In the secular world many have natural leadership abilities, but they know nothing about spirituality, therefore you cannot say unsaved people have the gift of shepherding.

MARY MAGDALENE

"Now it came to pass, afterward, that He went through every city and village, preaching and bringing the glad tidings of the kingdom of God. And the twelve were with Him, and certain women who had been healed of evil spirits and infirmities—Mary called Magdalene, out of whom had come seven demons, and Joanna the wife of Chuza, Herod's steward, and Susanna, and many others who provided for Him from their substance" (Luke 8:1–3).

Mary Magdalene is known by her hometown, i.e. Magdala, a small town south of Tiberias on the shore of the Sea of Galilee. There were two thriving businesses in this small little village. First, the "valley of the doves" began in the streets of Magdala and split the mountains, giving travelers passage from the Sea of Galilee up through the mountains to the small city of Cana. In that valley villagers trapped thousands of doves, selling them to the temple merchants to resell to worshipers who couldn't afford the price of a lamb or ox to sacrifice to God. Second, Magdala was known for the cultivation of the indigo plant used for dying cloth. There was a large cloth industry in Magdala.

In one of Jesus' first trips through Magdala (He would have gone through the town many times in His preaching tours of Galilee), Jesus cast seven evil spirits out of Mary and healed her of some physical illness. The Bible does not tell us what this illness was, but perhaps it was connected to demon possession.

From her worldly background and desperate condition, what qualified Mary Magdalene to be a shepherd? She had experienced the depths of sin and knew how addictive it could be to individuals. She knew they couldn't break Satan's stranglehold of sin without the power of Jesus. She was willing to lead people to Jesus so He could do for them what He had done for her. As Mary Magdalene became a follower of Jesus, her relationship to Him qualified her to be a shepherd. "The twelve were with Him, and certain women... Mary called Magdalene, out of whom had come seven demons" (Luke 8:1–2).

How long after her conversion did Mary give evidence of her leadership gift? Apparently, when Jesus went on His preaching tours, there was a long entourage following Him. First were the twelve disciples who helped Him in ministry. Second, there were other disciples (probably the seventy disciples), some of whom helped Jesus while others were learning from Jesus. In the third group were women, with Mary Magdalene always mentioned first, implying that she was their leader. These women followed Jesus, helping Him in ministry, but especially helping to pay bills. We know this from the following explanation, "The Twelve were with Him, and some women . . . Mary (called Magdalene) . . . Joanna the wife of Cuza . . . Susanna; and many others. These women were helping to support them out of their own means" (Luke 8:1–3 NIV).

WHO FOLLOWED JESUS?

The twelve disciples.

Other disciples (probably the seventy).

Mary, a leader of the women.

A group of women who worked and supplied money.

When is the next time we see Mary's gift of leadership? When Mark the gospel writer describes the various groups of people at Calvary, he notes there are soldiers, Jewish leadership, the crowd of onlookers, and a group of women observing from afar. "There were also women looking on from afar, among whom were Mary Magdalene, Mary the mother of James the Less and of Joses, and Salome, who also followed Him and ministered to Him when he was in Galilee, and many other women who came up with Him to Jerusalem" (Mark 15:40–41). Mary Magdalene's name was again mentioned first, suggesting she led a group of women to the crucifixion of Jesus. As the blood was dripping from the body of Jesus, and His life was being snuffed out on the cross, this group of devoted women watched from a distance. They couldn't do much, but they came to do what they *could.*

Where was the next location that Mary led them? Late Friday afternoon the body of Jesus was taken down from the cross, and Joseph of Arimathea took it to a nearby garden for burial. Joseph had a new tomb recently carved out of the rock in preparation for his burial. Jesus was buried in this borrowed tomb. But even then, a group of women watched where He was buried. Again the leader was mentioned first: "Mary Magdalene and Mary the mother of Joses observed where He was laid" (Mark 15:47).

Where did Mary next exercise her leadership? Early on Sunday morning, Mary led a group of women out to the garden where Jesus had been buried. They were bringing myrrh and incense to properly prepare His body for burial. But as the ladies got closer to the tomb, they were fearful of meeting Roman soldiers in a secluded spot, such as this garden. They had heard rumors of soldiers mistreating or raping women when caught alone. When the women arrived, it was not fully day; the shadows of the night lingered under the trees and darkness hid under the bushes. "As the first day of the week began to dawn, Mary Magdalene and the other Mary came to see the tomb" (Matt. 28:1).

Mary Magdalene suggested that she go spy out the garden to see what the Roman soldiers were doing. After all, she had been a woman of the streets—demon-possessed—so she didn't much care what happened to her. Mary Magdalene was concerned about the purity of the other Jewish women; she herself had little to lose. When she got close to the garden, she separated the dark leaves and realized that the soldiers were gone. There was no one there. The stone was rolled away from the door, and what little she could see in the tomb revealed that the body was gone. Mary mistakenly assumed that someone had stolen the body of Jesus, so she began running quickly toward the home of James and John to tell them what happened. In her excitement, she forgot about the other ladies waiting back in the darkness for her to come and tell them what she saw. Mary ran another way into the city to tell James and John what happened.

In piecing together the different gospel accounts, we see that while Mary was running away, the women finally got worried—or impatient—and they, too, came to the clearing in the garden and saw no one. It is then that the angel spoke to the women giving them the invitation, "Come, see the place where the Lord lay. And go quickly and tell His disciples that He is risen from the dead" (Matt. 28:6–7). The ladies ran off to obey the angel.

In the meantime, Mary Magdalene ran to the home of John and Peter, telling them, "They have taken away the Lord out of the tomb and we do not know where they have laid Him" (John 20:2).

Peter and John ran to the tomb, leaving Mary at their home, partly because she was winded and tired from her long run.

Peter and John ran to the tomb, examined it, and saw the grave clothes in their original condition, but they saw no corpse. The napkin that was about Jesus' head was folded and lying in another place. It is here that John was the first to realize that Jesus was raised from the dead, and he believed.

After Peter and John left the tomb, Mary got her breath and returned to the garden tomb. It is there that she finally looked in the tomb, where two angels sat. They asked her why she was weeping and she said it was because someone had stolen Jesus' body. Immediately, she sensed another person behind her, and, turning, she saw the person she thought was the gardener. She told Him, "If You carried Him away, tell me where You have laid Him, and I will take Him away" (John 20:15). It would have been physically impossible for Mary to move the body of Jesus with its heavy anointing of spices and oils; nevertheless her deep love motivated her to make such a plea. The Gardener had to say only one word to convince her who He was, "Mary."

Mary fell at Jesus' feet calling him, "Rabboni."

Because Mary had the gift of leading and influencing others, Jesus gave her a unique commission.

"Go to My brethren and say to them, 'I am ascending to My Father and your Father, and to My God and your God'" (John 20:17). She obeyed Jesus and returned to tell the apostles what she had seen and heard.

After this, Mary Magdalene is not mentioned again by name in Scripture. However, most scholars believe she gathered with the church in the Upper Room to fast and pray for ten days before the Holy Spirit came upon them at Pentecost. The Bible says, "These all continued with one accord in prayer and supplication, with the women [Mary Magdalene included] and Mary the mother of Jesus, and with His brothers" (Acts 1:14).

Mary was the leader among women when there were only women present. When women gathered with men to pray, she became one of the most fervent prayer warriors for God.

BEFORE THE CROSS	IN THE UPPER ROOM
Mary . . . A leader among women.	Mary . . . A prayer warrior with men.

PRACTICAL TAKE-AWAYS

The following questions were written for group discussion with a Sunday school class or Bible study. These questions are written in the first person to help you personalize your answers and apply them to your life.

1. *How can I know if I have the giftedness to be a shepherd?* Your first qualification for the gift of shepherding is knowing Jesus Christ and having a passion to lead individuals or a group to Him. If people naturally look to you, if you automatically influence their thinking, if you point them toward Jesus Christ, if you help them become more spiritual, this indicates you have the gift of shepherding. What you do with this giftedness depends on you. When others look to you, but you draw back from leadership responsibility, then your gift will decline or die. The way you encourage your leadership will determine if your gift will grow.

Some women want to be leaders. They volunteer for positions, or they push themselves into positions of leadership. If you do this, you may find followers whispering or complaining behind your back. If you've pushed yourself into a leadership position, don't automatically resign. First, you can work with the other women to get them to like you and follow you. Second, you can do a good job that will earn their respect. Third, you can grow your gift of shepherding/leadership. You can turn a difficult situation into a delightful ministry.

2. *After others decide to follow me, how can I continue being their leader?* Leaders continue to lead by decision-making. As a matter of fact leaders must make many decisions when they lead sheep. If you find it easy to make good decisions for other people or individuals, you probably have the gift of leadership. However, some have this gift, but decision-making does not come easy. You can learn to make better decisions. No matter whether decision-making is easy or hard, if your decisions produce spirituality in your followers, you probably have the gift of shepherding.

3. *After I learn to make good decisions, what is my next task as leader?* Probably mercy-showing is a good gift to add to shepherding. If you care about the spiritual condition of a group, then you probably have the gift of shepherding. However, just because you have a passion for the spiritual condition of others doesn't mean your dominant gift is shepherding. You could be a mercy-shower or you could have the gift of helps. Both of these will support the gift of shepherding. Shepherds also might have the gift of teaching or have some other dominant spiritual gift such as exhortation. But caring for sheep is the dominant trait of shepherding.

WHAT THOSE WITH THE GIFT OF SHEPHERDING DO

She leads Bible studies, is president of the ladies organization, heads up the kitchen committee, organizes others to begin a new program, rallies support for special church days, and is superintendent of the Sunday school. She leads family devotions when her husband is unsaved. She is a camp counselor, a youth sponsor, and a mission team leader. She leads her children.

4. *Are there any other characteristics that will reveal if I am a shepherd?* Yes, if people naturally look to you as an example or role model, then you qualify as a leader. If other women look to you for spiritual answers, and they naturally respect you, then you probably have the gift of shepherding. Just as every Christian must follow Jesus Christ, everyone sometimes needs a human example to know exactly how Jesus would act, react, and make decisions. Notice what Paul said about his example, "Imitate me, just as I also imitate Christ" (1 Cor. 11:1). In another place he said, "The things which you learned and received and heard and saw in me, these do, and the God of peace will be with you" (Phil. 4:9).

5. *I don't think of myself as a leader. Could I have the gift of shepherding?* Yes! Because all believers have been commanded to influence others to follow Jesus Christ, all women have the gift of shepherding. That includes you. Also, because every Christian has Jesus indwelling his heart, so the Lord influences others through you. Finally, since every Christian has the indwelling Holy Spirit and He is the authority behind every gift, including the gift of shepherding, then all believers are shepherds.

6. *Can I grow my shepherding ability?* Paul exhorted Timothy to grow his leadership ability, "Let no one despise your youth, but be an example . . . give attention to reading...to doctrine. Do not neglect the gift that is in you" (1 Tim. 4:12–14). Timothy was young and still growing, but Paul told him not to neglect his gift and to be about the work of ministry. It was doing ministry that caused Timothy to grow. So you will grow your gifts as you use them in ministry. Maybe you couldn't cook well when you got married, but you became a good cook by cooking. Therefore, you can heed the exhortation to Timothy; you can grow your gift as you are about the work of ministry.

THREE-STEP BIBLE STUDY

The following questions were written for group discussion with a Sunday school class or Bible study. These questions are written in the first person to help you personalize your answers and apply them to your life.

1. Who is the ultimate shepherd of the sheep?

> "The LORD is my shepherd" (Ps. 23:1). "I am the good shepherd" (John 10:11). "Jesus . . . . that great Shepherd of the sheep" (Heb. 13:20).

_____

_____

_____

2. If Jesus is our Shepherd, why do people need human shepherds?

> "When he [Jesus] saw the crowds, he had compassion on them, because they were harassed and helpless, like sheep without a shepherd" (Matt. 9:36 NIV).

_____

_____

_____

_____

3. **What is the secret a shepherd uses in leading others?**

"You in Me, and I in you" (John 14:20).

_____

_____

_____

4. **How can we grow our shepherding ability? Paul exhorted Timothy to grow his leadership ability.**

"Let no one despise your youth, but be an example . . . give attention to reading, to exhortation, to doctrine. Do not neglect the gift that is in you." (1 Tim. 4:12–14).

_____

_____

_____

5. **What two things does a leader of a flock do for sheep? How can you do this?**

"Therefore take heed to yourselves and to all the flock, among which the Holy Spirit has made you overseers, to shepherd the church of God which He purchased with His own blood" (Acts 20:28).

_____

_____

_____

6. **What are some things a shepherd should avoid?**

"Shepherd the flock of God which is among you, serving as overseers, not by compulsion but willingly, not for dishonest gain but eagerly" (1 Peter 5:2).

_____

_____

_____

7. **What is promised to shepherds?**

"When the Chief Shepherd appears, you will receive the crown of glory that does not fade away" (1 Peter 5:4).

_____

_____

_____

YOUR TIME TO PRAY

Add the following requests to your daily prayer list. As you pray about developing the gift of shepherding, you will find several things happening in your life: (1) Prayer gives you a desire to use your gift; (2) prayer gives you wisdom to use your gift (James 1:5); (3) prayer influences the lives of those you touch in ministry; (4) God answers by growing your gift: and (5) You grow to maturity in Christ and become more effective in use of all gifts.

1. *If you are not satisfied with your shepherding ability, ask God to grow your gift of leading others.* Lord, make me into a better leader.

2. *To be a leader, you have to think like a leader. Ask God to give you the mental ability to lead.* Lord, teach me what I don't know, and help me do what I can't, so I can better lead others.

3. *Leadership involves, first, knowing Christ, second, knowing yourself, and, third, knowing others.* Lord, I want your leadership to flow through me. Help me know my strengths and weaknesses, and help me understand those I will lead.

4. *A shepherd/leader must be committed to Jesus Christ to lead others to spiritual growth.* Lord, I yield my leadership gift to You. I will say what You tell me, I will follow where You lead me, and I will be what You want me to be.

5. *Since a leader must be an example to followers, ask God to use your testimony in the lives of your followers.* Lord, help me to be all that a leader should be, and help me to be an example to my followers and use my testimony in their lives.

6. Your personal prayer list:

   _____

   _____

   _____

   _____

   _____

   _____

JOURNALING AND MEDITATION

As you study this workbook, think about the things you are learning by writing them down. You will clarify your thoughts as you express them in words. Journaling turns feelings into acts and helps you understand what's happening internally. Actually, your journal—like a diary—is like a mirror that helps you look into your soul.

1. Name the woman you think is/was the greatest Christian leader since Paul the apostle. Why did you choose her? What does her example say to you? What can you learn about leadership from her?

2. What Christian female leader living today do you admire? Why did you choose her? What does her leadership example say to you? What can you learn from her?

3. Think of the female leaders in your church. Whom do you respect? Why? What have these women said to you?

4. If you were a better leader/shepherd, what ministry would you seek? Why?

5. Think about your goal of leadership. Write what kind of shepherd/leader you'd like to become.

6. Let's face it, some women are not much of a leader outside their family. Is that you? Why do you think you are weak in shepherd/leadership skills? Are you going to accept it as fact or do something about it? What? Why?

7. What journaling can look like:

Day One

Our friend, Doug Oldham, is a gifted communicator as well as a favored gospel singer. Sometimes while sitting in a congregation, my thoughts and emotions are changed from laughter to tears by the way he "sets up" the next song. It amazes me when I realize he has the whole congregation in the palm of his hand. He expresses his spiritual gift of leadership through his talent of singing.

The storytelling skills of Ethel Barrett motivated large groups to action. She led people to laugh, cry and before we knew it, she led us to repent or love God more. Max Lucado can tell a single story with an unforgettable spine-tingling punch line. Everyone knows he's a natural leader as he leads us to a conclusion, and we know it's his spiritual gift because he leads us to God.

Some people are "one-to-one" people, while others seem to have the gift of an effective group leader.

Day Two

As I pray the Twenty-third Psalm every morning, I'm so thankful for my Shepherd. I want to be a guide to my grandchildren. I want to help show them life's green pastures and places where there are still waters. I want them to know they don't have to walk in fear, but rather trust His presence with them.

I've never met a shepherd of sheep, but I've known some dear ladies who were faithful shepherds in Sunday school and daily vacation Bible school and even in our neighborhood Bible study group.

8. Now, your turn to journal:

_____

_____

_____

_____

How to Find and Grow Your Gift

PRACTICAL SUGGESTIONS TO HELP YOU DISCOVER YOUR SPIRITUAL GIFT

Your spiritual gifts are like windows—both give you two views. You can look out on the world's window, or you can look inside a house through a window. First, you look out a window to see the world. When you find your spiritual gifts, you'll see things and opportunities you've never seen before because you're looking at everything through your spiritual gifts. Isn't that a wonderful reason to find what gifts you have, so you can see the world differently?

But you can also look inside a building through its windows. As you discover your gifts, you'll discover new things about yourself as you look inward. You'll find some strengths or some passions you didn't know you had. You'll discover exciting possibilities or ways you can serve the Lord, and with these, you will find new satisfaction.

WINDOWS TO MINISTRY

Several years ago, we were house hunting and had almost exhausted the possibilities in our price range. One day the realtor called with news of "the perfect house." "It has the kinds of windows you like," she said. She was right! From the large oval window in the front door to the two-story, floor- to-ceiling windows in the living room, we were "sold" at first sight.

Windows come in all shapes and sizes. We have skylights, beveled glass, windows that slide sideways, and whole walls of windows. Some homes have casement windows, jalousie windows, bay windows, octagonal windows, garden windows, and stained-glass windows. Some windows are for special purposes, such as storm windows. Ticket windows have little holes in them, and tinted windows are installed in cars.

We face a new millennium in which women are no longer limited to a few windows of opportunity, but are only limited by their vision. Your spiritual gift is your window to ministry. Find your gift and serve the Lord joyfully. You'll look at everything differently.

By now you have read the previous nine chapters that describe each of the different spiritual abilities that God gives to His followers. So now you should have two questions:

A WINDOW TO VIEW MY GIFTS

1. What are my dominant spiritual gifts? (What can I do?)

2. How strong are my spiritual gifts? (How well can I do it?)

These two questions will be answered as you study the following suggestions. To discover your gifts, read each suggestion, fill out the checklist with each suggestion, and apply the results to your life.

A. KNOW WHAT SPIRITUAL GIFTS DO

The previous nine chapters have described the nine task gifts that are generally believed to be gifts by the majority of Christians. We have focused our attention on the gifts given to all believers. While these spiritual gifts are given to all believers at conversion, some of these abilities are not immediately evident in some believers, but may come to light at a later time. Why do we believe that all believers have some ability with each gift? Because: (1) The Holy Spirit is the energy of all spiritual gifts, and all believers have the Holy Spirit; (2) the Bible was written to all to exhort us to do the work that is accomplished by each spiritual gift. (An honest God would not give us a responsibility without a commensurate ability; therefore, we must have all gifts.) The following chart lists the nine spiritual gifts that we have studied in this workbook. Remember, we said in the introduction that most Christians agree with this list of task gifts.

THE NINE TASK GIFTS

1. Evangelism: getting others to make a decision for salvation.

2. Helps: helping others by serving them.

3. Teaching: getting others to learn and grow.

4. Exhortation: motivating others to practical Christianity.

5. Giving: furthering God's will by providing for needs of others.

6. Administration: managing people, money, resources, and time.

7. Mercy-showing: supporting others through problems.

8. Prophecy: defending justice and the honor of God.

9. Shepherding: leading individuals and groups for Christ.

Think again about our study of women with these nine spiritual gifts. In each chapter we included both biblical and modern-day stories of women with these spiritual gifts. Did you identify with some more than others? Was your heart kindled as you read? Did you find yourself praying to be used with certain gifts more than others? Now fill out the following checklist to assess what you think your strength is with each gift.

A WINDOW TO MEASURE YOURSELF

	I am strong in this area	I am average in this area	I am weak in this area
1. Evangelism			
2. Helps			
3. Teaching			
4. Exhortation			
5. Giving			
6. Administration			
7. Mercy-showing			
8. Prophecy			
9. Shepherding			

Obviously, your results on the previous chart may not be an accurate assessment; it is only your opinion. However, only you know what is in your heart, and your opinion is important. As an illustration, some women have had a desire to teach long before this ability was seen by others in the church. As a matter of fact, perhaps no one saw that she had the gift of teaching, and when she tried, she didn't do well. Her teaching gift was like a seed in the ground—embryonic—it came to life and grew later in life.

So your first step involves knowing what the Bible says about spiritual gifts. Just as you have difficulty finding something when you don't know what you're looking for, you will have difficulty finding your spiritual gifts if you are ignorant about them. Paul said about the gifts, "I do not want you to be ignorant . . ." (1 Cor. 12:1). So, the more you learn about spiritual gifts, the better you will be able to find out your strongest spiritual gifts and how to serve God with them.

B. KNOW YOUR DESIRE

When God gives a spiritual ability, He usually gives a desire to use the gift. If you have the gift of evangelism, you probably have a desire to see people come to Christ. Therefore, if you have a desire to serve the Lord in any way, begin praying that God would use you in that area. Be happy God has given you a "desire." Now express your desire to Him. "Delight yourself also in the Lord, / And He shall give you the desires of your heart" (Ps. 37:4).

A desire to serve the Lord is expressed in three ways. First, it is a burden. This has the meaning of "you know you must serve God in a particular way," or "you ought" to serve in that way. While a burden may have negative feelings to some who are resisting God, to others who are yielded to God, a "burden" to serve God feels good.

Second, a desire may feel like a passion or the positive feelings of love as "you love to help people." This desire was expressed by Jeremiah, "Your words were found, and I ate them, / And Your word was to me the joy and rejoicing of my heart" (Jer. 15:16).

Third, you express desires by excitement, laughter, or merriment. When exercising a spiritual gift that is obviously pleasurable, you probably not only have that gift, but it is probably one of your dominant gifts. A mercy-shower loves to talk to women—one-on-one—helping them through problems or to make decisions. What you like to do probably reflects your giftedness. The following checklist will help you look at your feelings to discover your giftedness. By assessing your desire with each gift, you may look at yourself objectively and discover your giftedness.

A WINDOW TO REVEAL YOUR EMOTIONS ABOUT SPIRITUAL GIFTS						
	Will not do	Fearful	Unsure	All right	Warm desire	Positive passion
1. Evangelism						
2. Helping						
3. Teaching						
4. Exhortation						
5. Giving						
6. Administration						
7. Mercy-showing						
8. Prophecy						
9. Shepherding						

Again, let me caution you about your negative feelings—they change. You may be fearful about witnessing today, but that can change. You may grow in Bible knowledge and, as you pray for someone to be converted, your passion for evangelism may grow. While your assessment on this chart may be misleading, remember two things: First, what you desire to do *may* be God's enablement. Second, what you don't want to do can change with time.

Now let's look at your positive feelings. You may mislead yourself about what you like. You may "push" the spiritual gift of teaching because your favorite friend is a teacher and you admire her greatly. There have been women who went to college to get a teaching degree, only to find out they didn't like it once they began teaching.

A WINDOW TO LOOK AT YOUR DESIRES

1. What you like to do *may* indicate God's giftedness for you.
2. What you don't like *can* change with time.
3. Look to God for His leading today, so you can grow in future service.

C. DEVELOP YOUR SPIRITUAL GIFTS BY USING THEM

Recently I attended a bridal shower where the bride-to-be received a wide variety of wonderful gifts. Some were practical, serviceable, and useful on a daily basis. Others were precious, lovely, fragile, or special occasion gifts.

When God gives us gifts He expects us to use them, not put them on a shelf to admire from a distance. Gifts gain value as we use them, and God increases their usefulness in and through use.

It may be that you do what is needed at your church simply because it needs to be done. That's wonderful. Most who have read this book have served because we wanted to or because we were asked. There was no thought of spiritual giftedness. God was glorified by your service and the work of Christ was done. But what most don't realize is that we grow as we serve Christ. As servants of the Lord we want to do our best, and as we strive for excellence, we become better. Just as we become stronger with more exercise, so our gifts become stronger the more we use them.

A WINDOW TO TELL WHAT HAPPENS WHEN YOU USE YOUR SPIRITUAL GIFTS

1. Christians grow to be like Jesus.
2. Listeners are convicted of sin.
3. Learners grow in Christ.
4. Sin's shackles are broken.
5. God is worshiped.
6. People are called into ministry.
7. Sinners are saved.
8. The body of Christ grows.
9. The work of Christ goes forward.

D. DO EVERYTHING AT HAND

The majority of believers throughout the history of the church have served God by doing what needed to be done and have been happy doing what God led them to do. That's wonderful! So don't wait to perform a ministry because you are not sure it doesn't match your giftedness. There's no verse in the Bible that tells you to do that. As a matter of fact, the opposite is taught, "And whatever you do, do it heartily, as to the Lord, and not to men" (Col. 3:23). So, begin now doing the ministry that's close at hand and needs doing.

A WINDOW ON WHAT TO DO

You—try to do all the things you can.
God—will take care of the fruit.

Three things will happen to you as you do what is at hand. First, you will gravitate to those ministries where you serve best. Second, you will discover what ministry you enjoy doing most. Third, your spiritual gifts will begin to emerge, first in your awareness, and second, others will notice and recognize your giftedness. Therefore, you'll find your giftedness as you serve the Lord.

As you try to do everything you can for the Lord, you will have some fruit in areas where you are best gifted. God will grow fruit through you. But there is something more important than growing your gift. As you try to do everything, God is growing you; and that's the most important thing. You are becoming like Jesus Christ. What should be your prayer?

A WINDOW OF PRAYER

Lord, use me according to my usability that I may become like You.

E. SETTLE DOWN TO DOING WHAT YOU DO BEST

Usually the ministers of our small churches end up doing everything in the church. They usually exercise all of the gifts, at least some of the time. In small churches the ministers don't have staff members to help them, so as shepherds they usually end up doing everything for their sheep. They do most everything in the church until they train others to help them. But what about you? You're not a pastor of a church, so here's what we suggest: "Do everything you can until you find what you do best, then settle down to do it for the glory of God."

If you have been serving the Lord, fill out the following checklist. If you are a new believer, or one who has not been active in Christian ministry, don't fill it out. You may not have the background to make a useable choice. But those who have spent a good deal of time in church will have some good ideas of their strengths.

A WINDOW TO SEE YOUR THREE STRONGEST GIFTS

	GIFTEDNESS/STRENGTH	REASONS FOR MY CHOICE
1.		
2.		
3.		

F. TALK TO A FRIEND

There comes a time when you talk to a friend or coworker about your abilities. Sometimes they may have been sizing you up as you were serving the Lord. They were not criticizing you, nor was it their intent to tear you down. Your friends know where you are strong and what is ineffective for you. And because they are friends, they'll help you, not hurt you.

The Scriptures tell us "in a multitude of counselors there is safety" (Prov. 24:6 KJV). So when two or three of your friends tell you the same thing about your strengths, listen to them. Pray about their advice; ask God to help you see yourself through the eyes of your friends.

Also, your friends can help you improve and grow your gift, "As iron sharpens iron, so a man or woman sharpens the countenance of a friend" (Prov. 27:17, author's paraphrase). This means that a friend can help you see yourself and develop your abilities. Think of a dull knife. It is harder to slice tomatoes with a dull knife than with a sharp one. Sharpening your tools, whether they are scissors, lawnmower blades, or Sunday school teaching skills, can increase production and help you do a better job.

A WINDOW INTO THE OPINION OF OTHERS

RELATIONSHIP	WHAT THEY THINK IS YOUR STRONGEST GIFT
MOTHER	
FATHER	
SPOUSE	
CLOSEST FRIEND	
PASTOR	
SUNDAY SCHOOL TEACHER	

Listen carefully to the positive comments of your friends. Many of your best friends won't comment on your weaker skills because they may think it's criticism. They don't want to hurt you, but even more importantly, they want to remain your friend. They feel negative criticism will injure their relationship to you. Fill out the following checklist before you talk to your friends. Write down what you think they will say is your strongest spiritual gift.

G. LOOK AT YOUR TRACK RECORD

Sometimes when you're lost and you can't see the sun or the horizon, look back. Looking in the rearview mirror will help you locate your present position. Most of us have 20/20 vision when it comes to looking in the rearview mirror. So when you look back or you see where you've been, it helps you plan for the next stop of your journey.

We've told you to try everything and to do what you do best. We've told you to talk to your friends to find out what they think you do best. Now we want you to go deep within your heart to find out something about your abilities. We're going to ask you to go deep within your memory. Make a list of ten tasks you've done for God in your life. This may take some time because some of you have forgotten a few things you didn't do well. You wanted to forget them. Well, resurrect them for a few minutes. Make a list of ten tasks, then put down a number to assess how well you think you did. Don't just think of your performance, think of results. How much did God use your ministry? What were the accomplishments?

A WINDOW ON PAST MINISTRY

LIST YOUR PAST MINISTRY	BEST				AVERAGE			POOR		
	10	9	8	7	6	5	4	3	2	1
1										
2										
3										
4										
5										
6										
7										
8										
9										
10										

Upon finishing this exercise, you should have a better idea of the areas of ministry where you get the best results. This may involve helping people come to Christ, or solving a problem, or getting through a crisis.

Compare this track-record chart with the previous chart on what gifts you desire to use. When both your desire and ability come together in a single gift, this area is probably a dominant spiritual giftedness of your life.

H. YOUR SPIRITUAL GIFTS WILL USUALLY BE REFLECTED IN YOUR NATURAL TALENTS

When God enters your life, He usually influences all of your personality. He begins at the core of your soul, and the conversion experience is so great that it oozes out to every part of your being. Among the many things God touches are your abilities or spiritual talents. This means that your spiritual gifts become evident through your natural talents and grow in spiritual effectiveness after you're saved.

Natural gifts are also called talents, such as musical talent, math talent, artistic talent, or journalistic talent. For the most part, these natural talents are inborn and the abundance of talents accelerates the endowed above and beyond the normal person.

Spiritual gifts are our abilities to do ministry for God, but it is actually the Holy Spirit working through us to produce spiritual results. Usually our spiritual gifts express themselves through our natural talents to do the work of God.

How do we know when a spiritual gift is operating? When we listen to a woman teaching the Word of God and she is only producing results that come from natural talent or natural training, we know very little, if any, spiritual gift is operative. When a woman teaches the Bible using both natural talents of speaking and her spiritual gift of teaching, there will be spiritual results.

Salvation is like a seed of life that is planted in your heart. "Therefore, if anyone is in Christ, he [she] is a new creation" (2 Cor. 5:17). Just as the seed of a new baby planted in a mother's womb will grow, so your new life in Christ will grow. This means your spiritual giftedness will grow after you are born again. Usually your spiritual abilities will follow the route of your natural abilities. If you are convinced about the things you do, and you naturally try to sell everyone else—you're like a salesman—you'll probably grow your spiritual gift of evangelism. The same with those who love to study new things and share them with others, they usually develop their spiritual gift of teaching.

Your spiritual giftedness and natural talents compliment one another. Another way to express it, "God uses people according to their usability."

Those with natural musical ability will probably use music to express their spiritual gift. Those who speak well in public are usually evangelists, exhorters, teachers, or pastors. Therefore, know yourself. Understanding your natural abilities *might* help you discover and develop your spiritual abilities.

IN A WINDOW OF YOUR NATURAL TALENTS

Understanding your natural abilities might help you discover and develop spiritual abilities.

Notice the word *might*. God in His sovereignty doesn't always match natural talents or abilities to spiritual gifts. God may use some people in an area where they have no *seeming* natural talents. There are many ministers who were bashful, shy, or had difficulty speaking in public. Yet, after conversion, God gave them the gift of public evangelism or teaching. Why would God do that? "But God has chosen the foolish things of the world to put to shame the wise, and God has chosen the weak things of the world to put to shame the things which are mighty" (1 Cor. 1:27). God may give a person a spiritual gift in an area where the person is weak, so that He gets the glory through the results of that gift.

However, most of the time, God matches natural talents with spiritual abilities. The following checklist is only suggestive of "Gift-Matching," i.e., spiritual gifts expressed through natural gifts.

A WINDOW ON MATCHING NATURAL TALENTS WITH SPIRITUAL GIFTS	
Public speaking	Exhorter
Desire to study	Teacher
Natural leader	Shepherd
Works with hands	Helps
Sensitive to others	Mercy-shower
Project Manager	Administration
Saleswoman	Evangelist
Analytical	Prophetess
Explains things	Teacher
Organizer	Administration
Handles money well	Giving

I. TAKE A SPIRITUAL GIFT TEST

The spiritual gift test at the end of this book will help you find your spiritual abilities. You will read and answer ninety questions. Your answers are designed to reveal your tendencies or strengths. Obviously, no test is absolutely accurate in every area, and this one will only be as accurate as the answers you give. Because we have difficulty understanding ourselves, we can't always answer accurately. But, because thousands have successfully used it, you can have confidence in its answers as it suggests areas in which you are strong or weak. It can be confidently used to guide you into ministry.

In the past thirty years, a number of spiritual gift instruments have been prepared and used by churches. Some of these have been extremely successful, such as the two million sales of *Spiritual Gift Inventory*, by Larry Gilbert (Church Growth Institute, 1-800-553-GROW). Another one that is extremely popular and immediately recognizable is *The Wagner Houts Spiritual Inventory*, by C. Peter Wagner (Gospel Light, 1-800-235-3475). The test at the back of this book was written by Elmer Towns, and thousands have been distributed free by

The Old Time Gospel Hour. If you want an electronic copy, visit www.elmertowns.com. After you take this test on your computer, it will automatically give you a profile of your spiritual gifts. If you want to take it with pen and paper, you may use the one at the end of this book. After you complete a profile of your spiritual gifts, it will help guide you into a more fruitful ministry. You may copy this test for use with a class or church.

REVIEW
HOW TO GROW YOUR GIFTS

A. Know what spiritual gifts do

B. Know your desire

C. Develop your spiritual gifts by using them

D. Do everything at hand

E. Settle down to doing what you do best

F. Talk to a friend

G. Look at your track record

H. Your spiritual gifts will usually be reflected in your natural talents

I. Take a spiritual gift test

PRACTICAL TAKE-AWAYS

This chapter has offered nine steps to helping you find and grow your spiritual gifts. However, the following practical principles can give you even more insight into serving the Lord.

1. *Must I take a spiritual gift test to find my giftedness*? Those who have been converted a long time and have spent a lot of time serving Christ probably have a good idea what their dominant spiritual gifts are without taking a test. They have learned by trial and error what their spiritual gifts are and what doesn't work for them.

2. *Can I serve Christ without knowing what my spiritual gifts are?* Most believers throughout the ages have successfully served Christ without ever wondering what their gifts were, or knowing anything about giftedness. They loved Christ, served Christ, and did whatever they found to do. God blessed them and used them, and they went to Heaven without ever knowing much about spiritual gifts. No, you don't need to know your gifts to serve Christ, but remember what Paul said about gifts, "I do not want you to be ignorant" (1 Cor. 12:1). When you know your gifts, you'll probably be more confident, effective, and happy in your service.

3. *I've just heard about spiritual gifts. Why is there so much emphasis today on spiritual gifts?* Why has so much knowledge about spiritual gifts and the appearance of spiritual gift testing only begun to appear in the past fifty years? Maybe the answer has to do with the kind of world in which we live. We live in a technical age in which we measure everything and give number to experience. "Hey Frank, that worship song is a ten!" The teaching about our gifts was always in the Bible, we've just applied it to the technical expressions of our times. This is not bad, since the Bible must always be applied to the life and times of its readers; we're just technical people applying God's Word to our high-tech world.

4. *What will I get most from studying spiritual gifts?* This book will help give you assurance about your abilities. Because of your study into spiritual gifts and taking the spiritual gift questionnaire, you can have confidence in your ministry. You can know in your heart that God will bless you as you obey His Word in ministry and use your dominant gifts. Also, you will understand why you have little results in some service, or why you don't enjoy some ministries as much as others. It's because of weak giftedness.

5. *What can I expect when I finish working through this book*? You will have a message of hope from working through this book. No matter who you are, no matter where you serve, and no matter what you do for God—you can do it better. You can grow in your giftedness and you can manifest spiritual gifts in your life that you haven't previously noticed. Paul tells us, "Earnestly desire the best gifts" (1 Cor. 12:31), so dream big. Paul also tell us, "Stir up the gift of God" (2 Tim. 1:6), so go do it better!

THREE-STEP BIBLE STUDY

Step One, read the questions to get you thinking about God's name.

Step Two, analyze the verses with each question to see what the Bible says about the question.

Step Three, write your answers in the space provided.

1. Who is the Giver of spiritual gifts?

"There are different kinds of abilities or gifts that come from the same Spirit. These gifts serve in different ways, but come from the same Lord. These gifts produce different results, but the same God does the work in everyone" (1 Cor. 12:4–6, author's paraphrase).

_____

_____

_____

2. What is the purpose of spiritual gifts?

"Each one should use whatever gift he has received to serve others, faithfully administering God's grace" (1 Peter 4:10 NIV).

_____

_____

_____

_____

3. Who has spiritual gifts?

> "*As everyone has received a gift, even so let them minister to one another*"
> (*1 Peter 4:10, author's paraphrase*).

_____

_____

_____

4. What can I do to increase my ability to minister (gifts)?

> "*Eagerly desire the greater gifts*" (*1 Cor. 12:31 NIV*). "*For this reason I remind you to fan into flame the gift of God, which is in you*" (*2 Tim. 1:6 NIV*).

_____

_____

_____

5. Can I have a dominant gift?

> "*Each one has his proper [unique] gift*" (*1 Cor. 7:7, author's paraphrase*).

_____

_____

_____

YOUR TURN TO PRAY

Add the following requests to your daily prayer list. As you pray about developing your gifts, you will find several things happening in your life: (1) Prayer gives you a desire to use your gifts; (2) prayer gives you wisdom to use your gifts (James 1:5); (3) prayer influences the lives of those you touch in ministry; (4) God answers by growing your gifts; and (5) you grow to maturity in Christ and become more effective in use of all gifts.

1. Ask God to bless your present ministry and grow your present gifts. Becoming stronger in ministry and the exercising of your present gifts is the basis for discovering new windows of service. *Lord, use me in ministry and help me find joy in what I do.*

2. If you're not involved in ministry, ask God to show you the ministry you would enjoy and would find profitable. Lord, I look within my heart to see what ministry would satisfy my desire to know You and serve You. Guide me in my search to find fulfillment in using my gifts.

3. Intercede for someone who you think has the same gifts as you, yet, like you, is not completely using her gifts. Lord, I pray for _____ that she would find her gifts and use them effectively for You.

4. Think about the ways you have effectively served Christ in the past. Then ask God to speak to you through your memory to help you find your most effective gift. Lord, help me remember where I've been the most effective so I can discover my dominant gift.

5. Pray that you understand what ministry you do best, so you can discover your dominant gift. Lord, show me my dominant gift so I can have confidence in serving You.

6. Ask God to give you insight as to whether your natural talents will help you discover your spiritual gifts. Lord, help me to see my natural talents as You see them and to use them spiritually, for Your ministry.

7. Your personal prayer list:

_____

_____

_____

_____

_____

_____

JOURNALING AND MEDITATION

As you study this workbook, think about the things you are learning by writing them down. You will clarify your thoughts as you express them in words. Journaling turns feelings into acts and helps you understand what's happening internally. Actually, your journal—like a diary—is like a mirror that helps you look into your soul.

1. The first way to find your spiritual gifts is to know them. Write your understanding of spiritual gifts.

2. Since another suggestion to find your gift is to serve in as many ways possible, make a list of the different types of ministry you've done.

3. Since you discover your giftedness by knowing what ministry gives you inward contentment, write a description of the ministry/gift that gives you the most fulfillment and why.

4. You probably have more than one opportunity for ministry before you at the present time (because all churches have need of workers). Write what you like about each opportunity and what you could accomplish through each.

5. Since natural talents and spiritual gifts go hand in hand, write a description of your natural talents. What have you learned from this exercise?

6. What journaling can look like:

Day One
Baby-sitting with grandchildren gives so much enjoyment and can yield some interesting insight into the personalities and talents of little ones.

Brad is inquisitive, with a need to take apart anything and put it back together with more than one leftover piece. He tilts his head to one side as if to say, "Now I wonder how that goes." He lines up trucks in a row, all even, all facing the same direction. Then, one by one, they are "driven" to the dumpsite then back. He's so much like his father, it's scary, because his dad at one time was a dispatcher for a trucking firm. I wonder how much of his talents he'll get from his dad and if he'll have the same spiritual gifts as his father.

Collyn, on the other hand, cares more about coloring a picture for Dad or creating a new recipe by combining all sorts of unusual foods, not normally eaten together. I see Collyn's mother with her creative, artistic talent. And I wonder about her spiritual gifts. Will they be the same as her mother's?

Day Two

I am to give spiritual ministry to others because God first gave me the gift of salvation, then He gave me the spiritual gift of service. We give gifts on birthdays and Christmas, also weddings or showers, are typical gift-giving events. But, is it wrong to have fun when you give gifts? Some of the most fun in giving a gift is an anonymous package left on the porch or a surprise "just because" present.

Our daughter, D. J., caught the "fun giving" idea while she was very young. At Christmas we chose to help a family who seemed to need a little help. We filled a box with food, toys, and clothing, then did what we called "drop, ring, and run," —drop the box on the front porch, ring the bell, and run!

Giving gifts also involved donating money so a child could go to camp or on a mission trip. Fixing a gift basket of goodies or giving time to help someone move are common "gifts" our daughters find pleasure in doing.

Giving is much more than a present delivered. It's an excitement within the giver and a deep satisfaction inside. You've given to others just as God has given to you.

7. Now, your turn to journal:

_____

_____

_____

_____

_____

_____

_____

_____

_____

_____

_____

_____

_____

_____

_____

_____

_____

_____

_____

_____

_____

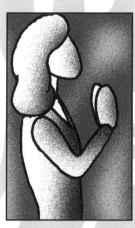

EPILOGUE

VESSEL UNTO HONOR

God is a magnificent chef who prepares wonderful meals and serves them in an exquisite manner. Everyone loves to eat at God's table because she gets the best food in the world, and all she wants. "You prepare a table before me . . . my cup runs over" (Ps. 23:5).

Sometimes God needs a big frying pan to cook a meal for multitudes of people. He reaches for a uniquely gifted woman with a capacity to do great things for the Lord. Right in the middle of the preparation, He needs a small pan to brown the gravy. He reaches for an unknown woman with a small gift. She is perfect for the task that God needs.

When it comes to vegetables, God doesn't need a frying pan, nor does He reach for the Crock-Pot; He needs a double boiler. He reaches for a woman with average gifts, but different from the frying pan. Next, He needs a small pot to steam a pan of fresh broccoli. There is a faithful woman in a small church, unknown to anyone but God; He reaches for her.

When God reaches for a platter for the meat, it's not big enough. This woman was given many gifts, but was not faithful in using them for God; she had not grown in her giftedness. So when God needed her for a special task, she wasn't ready. God had to use an old platter that didn't match the design of the other dishes. But the old platter was big enough because she had been faithful in the past.

God has all of His pots, pans, and dishes within reach. Each one can do a different job. Each one is a different size with varying capacities. They all look different and when you thump them with a finger, each makes a different sound. Some sing high, others are altos, and a few pewter pots go "clank." But God loves the sound of each one and He loves to use each one. But He can't use them if they're not ready.

What kind of vessel are you? Are you used of God every day or just on special occasions? Are you used for little girls' tea parties or does God use you to feed His army? Both are important, both are needed, both are used by God for entirely different reasons. Whatever you are, let God use you for His glory.

"In a comfortable home there are dishes made of gold, china, and crystal as well as some that are stoneware or others that are microwaveable. The expensive dishes are used for guests, and the everyday ones are used by the family. If you are a clean vessel, God can use you to fulfill His purpose in your life" (2 Tim. 2:20–21, author's paraphrase).

PARABLE OF THE TALENTED WOMEN

The president and owner of a realty corporation moved with her husband to a foreign country for a three-year assignment. The owner called in her longest-tenured and most talented saleswoman to give her a major role in managing the realty company while she was gone. The owner assigned the five commercial divisions to her trusted employee, giving her complete management of the commercial accounts while she was abroad.

Next, the owner called in her second-longest tenured employee, who was the next most gifted businesswoman. She entrusted the second employee with three divisions responsible for home sales.

Finally, the owner called in a young woman who had been with her for only one year. This new employee had only one talent. The owner gave her only one area to supervise, making her manager of the apartment rental section of the company.

The owner told all three women "to manage my business while I am gone and make it as profitable as possible. I will reward you when I return."

Three years later, the owner returned and called the employees into her office for a report. The owner asked the lady who had been with the business the longest. "What have you done with the five commercial accounts?"

"I invested the profits in new business accounts," she answered. "Now there are ten business accounts."

"Well done, faithful employee," the owner replied. "I'm putting $5 million in your retirement package."

The second employee stepped forward to report, "I have doubled the three divisions responsible for home sales; you now have six divisions of home sales."

"Well done, faithful employee," the owner replied. "I'm putting $3 million in your retirement package."

When the last employee came to report to the owner, she meekly said, "I knew you were a hard employer so I collected all the rent and kept it in a safety deposit box at the bank. Here is all your money—not a penny was lost."

"You are a foolish manager," the owner told the last woman. "Since you knew I was a hard boss, you could have expanded the business by purchasing more rental properties, or you could have put the money into a savings account so I could have at least gotten some interest."

The owner took the rental account away from the third woman and gave it to the first employee who had made the most money.

—Adapted from Matthew 2

BIBLIOGRAPHY

McDonald, Gail. *High Call, High Privilege*. Peabody, Mass.: Hendrickson Publishers, 1998.

LaHaye, Beverly. *I Am a Woman*. Old Tappan, N. J.: Fleming H. Revell Company, 1980.

Mains, Karen Burton. *Open Heart, Open Home: How to Find the Joy of Sharing Your Home with Others*. Elgin, Ill.: David C. Cook Publishing, 1976.

Pippert, Rebecca Manley. *Out of the Saltshaker and Into the World: Evangelism as a Way of Life*. Downers Grove, Ill.: InterVarsity Press, 1979.

TOWNS'S SPIRITUAL GIFTS QUESTIONNAIRE

STEP 1	GETTING READY TO GROW

GETTING READY TO USE THE SPIRITUAL GIFTS QUESTIONNAIRE

Using this questionnaire will not give you spiritual gifts, it will only reveal what spiritual gifts you already have and how strong they are. Taking this questionnaire will give you knowledge of how to serve God, and that is a powerful tool to change your life.

Pray and ask God to help you be as accurate as possible as you take this test. Keep an open mind as you read each statement. Don't react negatively, but answer according to what you think and do. Read each statement and answer as quickly as possible. Your first response is usually a truthful response.

The results about our spiritual giftedness are not final, so don't get discouraged with them. You are a growing believer in a growing church. Your ability to serve Christ can grow and it may change. This means you can strengthen your spiritual gifts, especially when there is a desire to do better. For those under age twenty, or those who have recently been saved, these answers may not accurately reflect your desire to serve Christ. You have not had time to learn your strengths and failures and you may not understand the meaning of "Christian" words used in this questionnaire. Until you know your limitations, you won't accurately know yourself nor will you accurately take this test.

When you get ready to interpret your abilities, notice your three strongest gifts. This is your *gift mix*. Don't look for just your strongest gift; study how one gift relates to the other.

Remember, God's plan is to "use you" where you are usable. This questionnaire will help you discover where you are most usable. When you know your gift, then place yourself at God's disposal to be used by Him.

STEP 2	WHAT ARE SPIRITUAL GIFTS?

This questionnaire only surveys the nine task gifts, also called the serving gifts. These nine spiritual gifts are generally recognized by evangelical believers. Different groups of believers add other abilities to their list that are not listed here, nor are they measured in this questionnaire. Because spiritual gifts should build unity in the body of Christ (1 Cor. 12:14–27), the obvious abilities usually taught by most evangelical churches are:

A. Prophecy

B. Helping

C. Teaching

D. Exhortation

E. Giving

F. Administration

G. Showing Mercy

H. Evangelism

J. Shepherding

STEP 3   EXPLAINING SPIRITUAL GIFTS

The following nine spiritual gifts used in the questionnaire are explained and illustrated to help you understand your spiritual gifts. Look up the scriptural references to help understand their nature and function.

PROPHECY: that special ability to see the influence of evil as did the Old Testament prophets and warn God's people of its damage. The prophet has a deep passion to defend God's reputation, stand for issues. She uses negative motivation, i.e., "so says the Lord . . ." (Rom. 12:6; 1 Cor. 12:10, 28; Eph. 4:11).

HELPING: that special ability to do service-oriented work for God in necessary tasks that may seem routine and mundane. The helper usually enjoys serving without public attention, doing such tasks as preparing a meeting room or working on a church building (Rom. 12:7; 16:1, 2; 1 Cor. 12:28; 1 Peter 4:10, 11).

TEACHING: that special ability and desire to study God's Word and share with others what is learned. The teacher enjoys communicating information to individuals or groups (Rom. 12:7; 1 Cor. 12:28; Eph. 4:11).

EXHORTATION: that special ability to find and communicate to others practical ways of serving God. The exhorter is a positive motivator, knowing practical Christianity will change the lives of others (Rom. 12:8; 1 Tim. 4:13; Heb. 10:25).

GIVING: that special ability to contribute material resources to God's work. The giver has a great desire to liberally share time, talent, and treasures with self-sacrificing cheerfulness (Rom. 12:8; 2 Cor. 8:1–7; 9:12).

ADMINISTRATION: that special ability to manage human, financial, and physical resources in an efficient manner. The administrator functions by planning, organizing, leading, and supervising (Rom. 12:8; 1 Cor. 12:28; Titus 1:5).

SHOWING MERCY: that special ability to empathize with those in distress to give spiritual comfort and support. The mercy-shower ministers by identifying with those in distress and comes alongside to lead them to wholeness (Matt. 9:36; Rom. 12:8).

EVANGELISM: that special ability to lead unsaved people to a knowledge of Christ. The evangelist has a passion for souls, a clear understanding of the gospel, and a tendency to be confrontational in approaching people because of the urgency of the task (Acts 8:5–6; 21:8; Eph. 4:11; 2 Tim. 4:5).

SHEPHERDING: that special ability to lead a group of believers. The shepherd (group leader) has a desire to help the group determine its spiritual goal(s), provide direction as it moves toward the goal, and protect group members from harmful influences (Eph. 4:11–14; 1 Peter 5:1–3).

STEP 4

HOW TO SCORE YOUR SURVEY

INSTRUCTIONS:

1. Begin with prayer, asking God to give you wisdom to be as accurate as possible.

2. Begin by reading statement 1, then determine your agreement with the statement. If the statement perfectly describes you, mark a "10," if it doesn't at all, mark "1." Most answers fall between these numbers, as no one perfectly expresses any gift and no one is devoid of any gift.

	Weak				Average				Strong	
	1	2	3	4	5	6	7	8	9	10

Keep an open mind, even if you react negatively. When you disagree with a statement, try to determine how much of the statement you can affirm.

3. Try to complete the entire questionnaire in one sitting (approximately 20 to 30 minutes).

4. Instructions for grading [steps 6 to 8] are found at the end of the questions.

5.

	Weak			Average				Strong	
1	2	3	4	5	6	7	8	9	10

1. Pray for unsaved people by name. **5**
   (If you only pray for them occasionally,
   write 5).

2. I look forward to speaking in public. **1**
   (If this terrifies you, write 1)

STEP 5

ANSWERING THE QUESTION. . .

	Weak			Average				Strong	
1	2	3	4	5	6	7	8	9	10

1. I believe in taking a stand on issues, even when no one stands with me, or even cares.		A
2. If a job is worth doing, it's worth doing well, and I can do it many times.		B
3. I can effectively motivate others into Christian service.		C
4. I enjoy studying the Bible to find new things.		D
5. I find tithing my income is easy to do.		E
6. I believe in managing money properly to get the most done, not spontaneous buying.		F
7. I want to spend more time helping addicted people break their habits.		G
8. I have shared my faith with many nonbelievers at school and/or work.		H
9. In a group, people look to me for leadership.		I

10.	The church would be stronger if pastors boldly denounced sin by name from the pulpit.		A
11.	I enjoy doing the little jobs around the church that others don't do.		B
12.	I think living an effective Christian life is more important than knowing doctrine.		C
13.	I take time from other things to study the Bible.		D
14.	I enjoy managing my money, paying bills, and writing checks.		E
15.	I believe most of the problems in our church come from poor management.		F
16.	I want to make sure everyone visiting my church is made comfortable.		G
17.	I find deep satisfaction when I lead someone to pray to receive Christ.		H
18.	I usually try to persuade members of my group to my point of view.		I
19.	If the church took a firmer stand on issues, society could be more righteous.		A
20.	I don't mind being asked to do something that takes time.		B
21.	People constantly tell me how much I have helped them in life.		C
22.	I can speak in public without embarrassment.		D
23.	I get great joy in writing out my weekly check for my church.		E
24.	I don't believe in doing a job that I can delegate to others.		F
25.	I want to spend more time helping addicted people break their habits.		G
26.	I have led many to Christ in my lifetime.		H
27.	I study practical ways to help the spiritual lives of others.		I

28.	I find it easy to confront inactive or uninvolved Christians.		A
29.	I like to help behind the scenes, without recognition.		B
30.	I think preaching should encourage listeners to healthy attitudes and practical living.		C
31.	I enjoy studying the meaning of words in the Bible.		D
32.	I am ready to give additional finances for special evangelistic crusades.		E
33.	I believe we could get more done if we planned and followed a detailed schedule.		F
34.	I enjoy ministering to discouraged believers to motivate them to overcome their problems.		G
35.	I find it natural to turn the conversation with unbelievers toward my church or Lord.		H
36.	I find it easy to make a decision for the people in any group I am with.		I
37.	When church members try to hide their sin, I feel a pastor should rebuke them.		A
38.	When I serve the Lord, I don't care who gets the credit.		B
39.	I can effectively motivate others into Christian service.		C
40.	I spend extra time studying my Bible because I love to teach.		D
41.	I look for items in my budget to cut back, so I can give more to God.		E
42.	I usually think of a long-range plan for projects before others see it.		F
43.	I am willing to assist others to make the ministry go forward.		G
44.	I am so convinced that people are lost, I try to communicate the gospel even though people resist.		H
45.	I have a concern that people in my group grow in Christ.		I

46. I believe in confronting a friend about a non-Christian attitude.	A
47. I get more pleasure out of doing a job well than from compliments.	B
48. I enjoy sermons with positive suggestions more than those that attack sin.	C
49. I believe that it is terrible to speak in public without having something to say.	D
50. I am not offended when the church asks for extra money for foreign missions.	E
51. I believe the church needs more job descriptions to get more done for God.	F
52. I feel so deeply about cancer victims that I want to be with them in their need.	G
53. Because I love to share my faith with unsaved people, I get frustrated at Christians who don't.	H
54. I am so concerned when people drop out of my group, that I go after them.	I
55. I am not embarrassed to wear a religious pin or read my Bible in public.	A
56. I appreciate the opportunity to do any task to help the ministry.	B
57. I like to share some practical helps that will make life easier to live.	C
58. My greatest satisfaction is helping others get new insights from the Bible.	D
59. I get irritated when my church has a money need and doesn't ask me.	E
60. I believe it is important to plan small details so a group won't waste time.	F
61. I feel the sufferings of people so deeply that I try to help them.	G
62. I am always inviting unsaved people to attend church because I want them to be converted.	H
63. I try to get my friends together for fellowship or to serve Christ.	I

64.	I feel we need more preaching on sin—"calling a spade a spade."	A
65.	I want to give extra time to do any little job at the church.	B
66.	I would rather hear practical sermons than negative ones that attack.	C
67.	I have not taught an acceptable lesson unless I share some new truth from the Word of God.	D
68.	When I've increased my tithe, God has blessed me financially, so I constantly look for extra ways to give more money.	E
69.	I like everything in its place, and everything cleaned up before I can relax.	F
70.	I find my deepest reward when discouraged people are helped by my support.	G
71.	I look forward to presenting the gospel to the unsaved when the church invites me to participate in evangelistic outreach events.	H
72.	I will give up personal time to help everyone in my group become obedient to Christ.	I

73.	To help people, I don't allow them to feel comfortable in their sin, but I confront their sin.	A
74.	I feel good when a job is done right; no one has to compliment me.	B
75.	I tend to enjoy sermons with practical applications more than "deep" sermons.	C
76.	I think knowing the Bible doctrine is more important than learning practical helps.	D
77.	I begin with the tithe and then give extra.	E
78.	I believe our church would be better if we followed more carefully the master calendar, the budget, and the bylaws.	F
79.	People tell me their problems because I understand and support them.	G
80.	The main problem with my church is many members are not interested in soul-winning.	H
81.	I pray for many in my group, because they don't pray for themselves.	I

82.	I feel confident telling others what to believe about the Bible and correcting their wrong views.	A
83.	I appreciate the opportunity to do any task to help the ministry.	B
84.	Everyone in the church can be helped with a kind word, so be slow to criticize.	C
85.	I enjoy taking the responsibility for the growth of Bible knowledge in others.	D
86.	I believe we should give our money to God, even when we have to sacrifice necessities to do it.	E
87.	I believe we need more supervision of ministry so we would have better results.	F
88.	I try to be there when my friends need me—not to do something for them, but to spend time with them.	G
89.	People say I'm compulsive because I'm always trying to share Christ with them.	H
90.	Whenever I'm in a group of people, I usually take over leadership.	I

STEP 6

FINDING YOUR SCORE

Now you will add up your score to determine the strength of each of your spiritual gifts. Go through statements 1 to 90 and add the numbers of all items marked "A." There are ten items marked A. Put the total number below, next to "A" Prophet. Follow the same procedure for all, "A" through "I."

PROPHET   A _____   ADMINISTRATOR   F _____

HELPER   B _____   MERCY-SHOWER   G _____

EXHORTER   C _____   EVANGELIST   H _____

TEACHER   D _____   SHEPHERD   I _____

GIVER   E _____

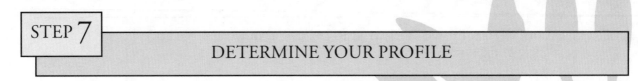

STEP 7

DETERMINE YOUR PROFILE

Write your total score for each of the above categories in the column marked "Total Score." Next, mark an "X" in the column which includes your scoring range as shown in the example that follows:

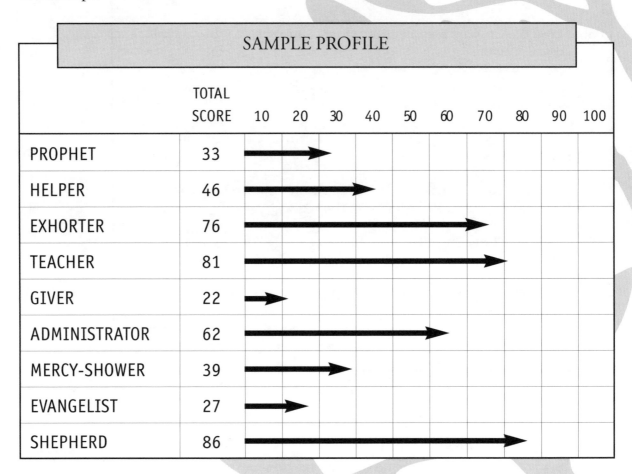

	TOTAL SCORE	10	20	30	40	50	60	70	80	90	100
PROPHET	33										
HELPER	46										
EXHORTER	76										
TEACHER	81										
GIVER	22										
ADMINISTRATOR	62										
MERCY-SHOWER	39										
EVANGELIST	27										
SHEPHERD	86										

SAMPLE PROFILE

SUGGESTED INTERPRETATION

The person above has three strong gifts, i.e., shepherd, teacher, and exhorter. This person has abilities to lead people as a shepherd, leading them by teaching in a group setting, and using positive and practical material in youth and adult classes, speaking at seminars or training sessions, or making reports to a committee. This person might be a pastor, and if so, would have teaching strength in the pulpit, but evangelistic weakness.

Because this person has low scores in mercy-showing, he or she might not be effective in teaching children, counseling, or helping individuals.

This person might not be effective in evangelism because of low scores in evangelism and prophecy.

This person might be a good manager of adult church programs.

STEP 8

CHART YOUR PROFILE

Now, take your totals and chart your own profile.

YOUR PROFILE

	TOTAL SCORE	10	20	30	40	50	60	70	80	90	100
PROPHET											
HELPER											
EXHORTER											
TEACHER											
GIVER											
ADMINISTRATOR											
MERCY-SHOWER											
EVANGELIST											
SHEPHERD											

STEP 9

INTERPRETING YOUR SPIRITUAL GIFTS

1. The chart (step 8) gives you the raw score of your spiritual gifts. You can interpret your scores according to these general principles:

2. The higher your score in an area (i.e., score 75 to 100), the more gifted you are in that gift.

3. Remember that laypeople tend to have lower scores than full-time workers, who tend to score high.

3. Don't be discouraged by a low score and don't give up your attempt to use that gift. You can grow in any ability or spiritual gift.

4. Watch for two or three highest gifts. Compare these strengths (called your "gift mix") to see how they work together. As an illustration, strength as a shepherd (group leader) and strength as a teacher means you will lead a group by teaching.

5. Concentrate on your strengths in serving Christ, not your weaknesses. Total Christian service will strengthen weak gifts, but don't focus all your energies on them.